BATTLE

THE RETREAT FROM
MONS, 1914:
SOUTH

Etreux to the Marne

PASSANT

ARRETE-TOI

The Cecil Memorial in the Forêt Domaniale de Retz.

THE RETREAT FROM MONS, 1914: SOUTH

Etreux to the Marne

*The Western Front
by Car, by Bike and on Foot*

Jon Cooksey
and Jerry Murland

Pen & Sword
MILITARY

First published in Great Britain in 2014 by
PEN & SWORD MILITARY
an imprint of
Pen & Sword Books Ltd
47 Church Street
Barnsley
South Yorkshire
S70 2AS

ISBN 978 1 47382 336 5

A CIP catalogue record for this book is
available from the British Library.

Typeset in Palatino and Optima by
CHIC GRAPHICS

Printed and bound in India by
Replika Press Pvt. Ltd.

Pen & Sword Books Ltd incorporates the imprints of
Pen & Sword Archaeology, Atlas, Aviation, Battleground, Discovery,
Family History, History, Maritime, Military, Naval, Politics, Railways,
Select, Social History, Transport, True Crime, and Claymore Press,
Frontline Books, Leo Cooper, Praetorian Press, Remember When,
Seaforth Publishing and Wharncliffe.

For a complete list of Pen & Sword titles please contact
PEN & SWORD BOOKS LTD
47 Church Street, Barnsley, South Yorkshire, S70 2AS, England
E-mail: enquiries@pen-and-sword.co.uk
Website: www.pen-and-sword.co.uk

CONTENTS

INTRODUCTION AND ACKNOWLEDGEMENTS

This guide – the second of two companion volumes – follows the route of the southern half of the fighting retreat of the British Expeditionary Force (BEF) over a distance of some 322km/200 miles from Mons in Belgium in August and September 1914 to points south of the River Marne in neighbouring France. The retreat from Mons lasted for thirteen exhausting days and despite the fact that, at the time of writing, it took place a hundred years ago; the landscape that witnessed the innumerable clashes between the British rearguards and the pursuing German Army has changed very little. Hailed as a magnificent feat of arms, it was a retreat from which the British emerged by the skin of their teeth. Today this historic route is marked only by the numerous small CWGC cemeteries and memorials which bear witness to the daily struggle between life and death during one of the longest retreats in the history of the British Army.

As with our previous guidebooks, this volume focuses on what the battlefields look like today and although you will find very few contemporary Great War photographs, the guide is profusely illustrated with selections from our own collections, many of which have been taken specifically for this book. The guidebook contains five routes which can be walked, biked or driven and which are supplemented by visits to twelve other sites where we describe what took place and why. When designing routes we have tried once again to ensure that vehicles are not left at isolated points, however, please take the usual sensible precautions with an unattended vehicle by not leaving valuables on display but by locking them securely in the boot. Coordinates are provided for the start of each route. On the majority of routes it is possible to cycle and walk, but on some of them cycling is either prohibited or is only possible with a good off-road bike. Where possible we have directed the battlefield tourist onto quiet and little-used minor roads as well as local pathways and cycle tracks but be aware that even on the quietest of rural roads there is always the likelihood of meeting unexpected farm machinery.

The depth of historical information devoted to each stage of the British retreat from Mons has, by necessity, been limited by available space but we have provided enough of an outline around which to develop your understanding of what took place and why. Nevertheless, we have made a number of suggestions for further reading which will widen your appreciation of the events that took place during the retreat. We also point readers in the direction of other useful guidebooks and publications which cover part or all of the retreat.

What is often confusing to the first-time battlefield tourist is the terminology used in describing the ranks and organization of the various armies of the Great War. In this volume we have provided a quick guide to the organization of the British Army in 1914 together with a comparison of the respective ranks of both armies. In acknowledging the assistance of others we must thank Hedley Malloch for his sage guidance with the route concerning Iron – along with the photograph of the Iron Memorial inauguration – and Yvon Debuire at Néry for his assistance with the L Battery material. We also extend our appreciation to Sebastian Laudan for his enormous efforts in translating German unit histories and his boundless enthusiasm while touring the ground with us.

A NOTE ON THE BRITISH ARMY OF 1914

The British Army that went to war in August 1914 was made up of entirely professional soldiers. It was the result of the reorganization undertaken after the embarrassment of the Boer War of 1899–1901 when the British Army was found wanting in the face of the irregular tactics of its Boer adversaries. In 1907 Richard Burton Haldane, the Secretary of State for War in the Liberal Cabinet of Sir Henry Campbell-Bannerman, began the task of reshaping the army to provide the Empire with a small but effective professional force which could both police the Empire and provide home security. While the army in the outposts of Empire was kept up to full strength by a regular flow of men from home bases, the home army was generally well below fighting strength.

An essential part of Haldane's reforms was the creation of the BEF consisting of six divisions, the ranks of which could be filled by the creation of a reserve – men whose time with the colours had expired but were contracted to remain available for call-up should a national emergency arise. Thus the army that left British shores to fight on the mainland of Europe for the first time since Waterloo relied heavily on reservists to bring it up to war strength. These men were supplemented by men of the Special Reserve, similar in many ways to the part-time soldiers of the Territorial Force which existed for home defence, in that they were essentially civilians who undertook regular periods of military training. But unlike the Territorials, they were liable for overseas service. It is estimated that 60 per cent of the BEF's manpower came from its reservists and it was these men who suffered the most due to problems arising from their lack of military fitness on the long march from Mons. However, they proved on numerous occasions that they had not forgotten how to 'soldier'. It was their professionalism and tenacity that won them the accolade 'The Old Contemptibles' as

The Irish Guards outside Wellington Barracks on mobilization.

they fought their way back from the Marne to the Aisne and then onto Ypres where they joined the 7th Division to fight the First Battle of Ypres in October 1914.

The basic formation of the British Army in 1914 began with the infantry platoon. Commanded by a second lieutenant or lieutenant and assisted by a platoon sergeant, it comprised about fifty men who were organized into four sections, each commanded by a corporal or lance corporal. There were generally four platoons in a company, all of which answered to a company commander, usually a captain or major. A total of four companies and a headquarters company made up a battalion, commanded by a lieutenant colonel. Within the headquarters company was the second-in-command, the battalion adjutant – the colonel's right-hand man – the regimental sergeant major and the battalion quartermaster. Usually the battalion medical officer was part of this group. The next unit of command was the brigade; this was initially made up of four battalions – in 1918 this was reduced to three – and in overall command was a brigadier general. A division consisted of at least three brigades and was commanded by a major general. Beyond that, divisions were organized into corps usually commanded by lieutenant generals and armies (generals) and all these formations were under the direction of the Commander-in-Chief. The cavalry was structured in a similar fashion, except that its constituent parts were known as troops, squadrons and regiments which were organized into cavalry brigades and divisions. Artillery units had batteries of guns which became brigades when grouped together and the Royal Engineers used the term sections and companies to describe their basic formations. The Royal Flying Corps organized their aircraft into flights and squadrons and later grouped squadrons into brigades.

RANKS USED IN THE BRITISH AND GERMAN ARMIES

It is always somewhat confusing when visiting German military cemeteries to try to understand the various ranks of the German soldiers buried there. To that end we have produced a rough guide to equivalent German and British ranks which should assist you when visiting the German cemeteries described in the guidebook.

British	German
Field Marshal	*Generalfeldmarschall* (honorary title)
General	*Generaloberst* (army commander)
General	*General der Infanterie/Kavallerie/Artillerie* (corps commander)
Lieutenant General	*Generalleutnant* (division commander)
Major General	*Generalmajor* (brigade commander)
Brigadier General	(There is no equivalent rank but on occasions a senior *Oberst* was charged with brigade command)
Colonel	*Oberst*
Lieutenant Colonel	*Oberstleutnant*
Major	*Major*
Captain	*Hauptmann/Rittmeister*
Lieutenant	*Oberleutnant*
Second Lieutenant	*Leutnant*
Warrant Officer	*Feldwebelleutnant*
Regimental Sergeant Major	*Offizierstellvertreter*
Company Sergeant Major	*Feldwebel* (or *Wachtmeister* in the cavalry or artillery)
Sergeant	*Vize-Feldwebel*

Corporal	*Unteroffizier/Oberjäger*
Bombardier	*Obergefreiter*
Lance Corporal	*Gefreiter*
Private	*Schütze/Grenadier/Jäger/Musketier/*
	Soldat/Gardist/Pionier/Füsilier/
	Kanonier/Fahrer/Infanterist

VISITING MILITARY CEMETERIES

The concept of the **Imperial War Graves Commission (IWGC)** was created by Major Fabian Ware, the volunteer leader of a Red Cross mobile unit which saw service on the Western Front for most of the period of the war. Concern for the identification and burial of the dead led him to begin lobbying for an organization devoted to burial and maintenance of those who had been killed or died in the service of their country. On 21 May 1917 the Prince of Wales became the president of the IWGC with Fabian Ware (1869–1949) as its vice-chairman which forty-three years later became the **Commonwealth War Graves Commission (CWGC)**. Neither a soldier nor a politician, Ware was later honoured with a knighthood and held the honorary rank of major general. The commission was responsible for introducing the standardized headstone which would bring equality in death regardless of rank, race or creed and it is this familiar white headstone that you will see now in CWGC cemeteries all over the world. The tall Cross of Sacrifice with the bronze Crusader's sword can be found in many cemeteries, such as Noyon New British Cemetery, where there are relatively large numbers of dead and can even be found in smaller ones such as the Guards' Grave Cemetery at Villers-Cotterêts, but generally in the smaller cemeteries, such as those at the churchyard at Doue, only the headstones mark the final resting place of the men who fell.

Major General Sir Fabian Arthur Ware.

CWGC cemeteries are noted for their high standards of horticultural excellence and the image of rows of headstones set amidst grass pathways and flowering shrubs is one every battlefield visitor takes away with them. On each headstone is the badge of the regiment or corps or in the case of Commonwealth forces, the national emblem. Below that is the name and rank of the individual and the date on which they died together with any decoration they may have received. Headstones of Victoria Cross winners also have the motif of the decoration on their headstone. At the base of the headstone is often an inscription which has been chosen by the family. Headstones marking the unidentified bear the inscription chosen by Rudyard Kipling, 'A Soldier of the Great War, Known Unto God', while special memorials are erected to casualties known to be buried in the cemetery but whose precise location is uncertain.

The pattern of Lieutenant Ames' headstone at Compiégne is of a standard pattern – the 'World War' pattern – across all First and Second World War CWGC cemeteries. Post-war CWGC headstones have a notch cut into either shoulder at the top.

In the area covered by this guidebook we have referred to and described over eighteen cemeteries containing British and Commonwealth casualties and eight French National Cemeteries. The majority of the British casualties are buried in small CWGC plots contained within local communal cemeteries, or in some cases, within French National Cemeteries. The presence of these casualties is marked by the familiar green and white sign at the entrance, with the words *Tombes de Guerre du Commonwealth*. In communal cemeteries the CWGC headstones are often separated from one another and in some cases, such as those in Etreux and Compiègne Communal Cemeteries, are hidden among the more elaborate French civilian gravestones. Where this is the case we have given directions to each of the casualties.

Tombes de Guerre du Commonwealth

Commonwealth War Graves

The distinctive dark green and white CWGC sign found at the entrance to communal cemeteries where British and Commonwealth casualties are buried.

A small CWGC plot at Baron Communal Cemetery.

In the larger cemeteries a visitor's book and register of casualties is kept in the bronze box usually by the entrance but in the smaller communal cemeteries scattered along the line of the retreat the register is kept by the cemetery *concierge* or at the local *mairie*.

French National Cemeteries

The numerous French National Cemeteries that you will come across are generally concentration cemeteries in that they often contain mass graves or *ossuaires*, comprising casualties brought in from a wide area or from a specific battle, such as that at Guise, in addition to individual graves. They are looked after by the **Ministere des Anciens Combattants et Victims de Guerre**. The cemeteries are generally signposted with a black and white sign with the words *Cimetière Militaire* and the French national flag flies daily at each location. Where there are individual headstones they usually take the form of concrete crosses each bearing a metal plate containing the military details of the man buried and the date of death; sadly many of them are now suffering from the effects of weathering.

French military cemeteries are usually clearly marked.

Headstones of North African and colonial troops have a more shaped outline, as do those for Jewish soldiers.

German Cemeteries

The German War Graves Commission – **Volksbund Deutsche Kriegsgräberfürsorge** – is responsible for the maintenance and upkeep of German war graves in Europe and North Africa. The German cemeteries are in stark contrast to the CWGC cemeteries in that they often exude a dark and sombre ambiance. The grave markers lack standardization and vary in style from cemetery to cemetery. Like many French cemeteries, they often contain mass graves for the unidentified and headstones can carry up to three or four names on each one. We would recommend you visit German cemeteries where possible as they can

French colonial casualties from North Africa have distinctively shaped headstones.

provide the battlefield tourist with a greater understanding of the huge loss of life that occurred on both sides of the conflict.

HISTORICAL CONTEXT

After the French declaration of war on Germany on 3 August 1914, German troops crossed the border into Belgium at 8.02am the following morning, near the frontier town of Gemmerich. The German invasion strategy – the **Schlieffen Plan** – first formulated by **Count Alfred von Schlieffen** in 1905, had been organized to the last detail. Assuming a war against two enemies, France to the west and Russia to the east, it laid down the conditions for a swift, decisive and victorious incursion via neutral Belgium to defeat France, followed by a rapid shift of troops east to defeat a lethargic Russia.

Britain's declaration of war on 4 August 1914 followed Germany's blatant flouting of Belgian independence and neutrality which had been agreed by the European powers in the 1839 Treaty of London. Plans had long been in existence for the British to come to the aid of Belgium in the event of invasion by a hostile power, plans that now became manifest in the form of the BEF under the overall command of **Field Marshal Sir John French**. Compounded by fears in England of a German invasion of the home country and recent trouble in Ireland over Home Rule, the British Government was initially cautious,

Field Marshal Sir John French.

committing only four of its six available infantry divisions and one cavalry division to the BEF. Thus, the fighting strength of the British force that went to war was made up of I Corps (1st and 2nd Divisions) commanded by Lieutenant General Sir Douglas Haig, II Corps (3rd and 5th Divisions) commanded by **Lieutenant General Sir James Grierson** and a Cavalry Division under the command of **Major General Edmund Allenby**. In addition there were the five infantry

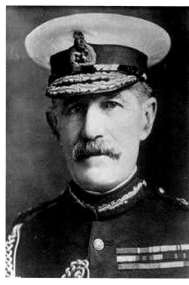

Sir Horace Smith-Dorrien.

Sir Douglas Haig.

Major General Edward Allenby.

battalions of 19 Brigade designated for the protection and maintenance of the lines of communication. Sadly Grierson died from a heart attack on the way to Le Cateau on 17 August and was replaced by **General Sir Horace Smith-Dorrien** two days later.

The BEF advanced into Belgium to take up their allotted position on the left of **General Charles Lanrezac's** French Fifth Army, a movement that coincided with the German First and Second Armies advancing from the northeast. Lanrezac, realizing the size of the enemy force approaching him, decided to retire on 22 August, leaving the BEF to face the German First Army along the line of the Condé Canal at Mons on 23 August. As the great mass of the German First Army – moving southwest – approached the canal, its troops were not expecting to meet resistance. But the British were in position. It fell to the 4/Middlesex Regiment dug in at Obourg to be the first unit to feel the full weight of the German IX Corps as its left flank vanguard arrived at the canal. Contact between the two sides then crackled along the length of the canal like a slow-burning fuse as more and more German units swung south to reach the line of the canal. The slow fuse of battle which had been lit at Obourg took several more hours to reach the 5th Division further west at St Ghislain.

There can be little doubt that the BEF gave a good account of itself at Mons but we should not underestimate the extent of the German achievement. By early afternoon of 23 August, initial German surprise at finding the BEF along the canal at Mons had quickly turned from what had begun as a route march into a successful encounter engagement. Moreover, elements of the German IX Corps had crossed the canal at several points, effectively rendering the already precarious 3rd Division positions in the Nimy salient completely untenable and putting the 5th Division further west under severe pressure. Despite the fact that the French Fifth Army had already retired south, the BEF were in danger of being caught in a German pincer movement.

It is now thought that the German casualty figures at Mons – approximately 5,000 killed, wounded or missing as originally recorded by British sources – were not nearly as high as first thought. A revised figure of 2,000 killed and wounded would be nearer the truth. As for the British casualties, a figure between 800 and 1,000 men killed in action is thought to be realistic. Another question mark hovers over the popular belief that German forces attacking at Mons were convinced that they were facing large numbers of British machine guns, an impression apparently reinforced due to the sustained and accurate rifle fire of the British infantry. There is little or no evidence to support this notion. Similarly British sources also hold fast to the belief that the British infantry cut the advancing 'grey hordes' down in their hundreds, a view that is at odds with the casualty figures recorded in German unit war diaries and histories.

With the orders to retreat relayed to corps commanders late on 23 August, the BEF fought its way south through the many mining villages and towns that lay on its route. Despite the 5th Division rearguard having to fight at **Audregnies** on 24 August, Bavay was reached by the bulk of both British corps by nightfall. South of Bavay the BEF split to pass either side of the **Fôret de Mormal**; Smith-Dorrien's II Corps moving down the western side of the forest to Le Cateau – where he was joined by the newly arrived 4th Division – and Haig's I Corps to the east, where the encounters at **Maroilles**, **Grand Fayt** and **Landrecies** took place. **Le Cateau** was fought by II Corps on 26 August without the support of I Corps which pursued a separate line of retreat until 1 September when the two 'halves' of the BEF were eventually reunited.

The saga of the retreat abounds with tales of rearguard gallantry as the BEF moved further and further south towards the Marne. Among those included in this guidebook are the heroic stand of 2/Royal Munster Fusiliers at **Etreux**, the 5 Cavalry Brigade action at **Cerizy**, the epic Guards Brigade fight in the forest north of **Villers-Cotterêts** and L Battery of the Royal Horse Artillery at **Néry**. After the crossing of the River Marne on 3 September events sped towards a conclusion. By 4 September French Commander-in-Chief General Joffre's plans for a counter attack were falling into place and he was then in a position to deliver a blow to the German invaders which he hoped would halt them in their tracks. The First Battle of the Marne was about to begin.

On Sunday 6 September the men of 17/Field Company, Royal Engineers, began their advance to the Marne and although he had only been in France for a short time, **Second Lieutenant Kenneth Godsell** felt it had been much longer. 'Three weeks since we left

Dublin – a fortnight since St Ghislain [Mons]. Today we make a step in the right direction.'

The *British Official History* records British casualties between 23 August and 5 September 1914 as a little over 15,000 – the majority of those being from units of II Corps – a shocking number until it is realized that casualties is a generic term that covers those killed, wounded, missing or taken prisoner. Quite literally a soldier is considered to be a casualty if he is missing from roll call and thus unable to be counted as an effective fighting man. In fact the number of British troops actually killed during the retreat was relatively light – although some battalions were hit harder than others in this respect. Where the BEF suffered most heavily was in the numbers of men taken prisoner, either after engagements such as Mons, Le Cateau and Etreux, or as a result of men being left behind on the march, exhausted, wounded or in some cases simply unwilling or unable to continue. Men became easily detached from their parent units in the confusion and were consequently posted as missing at roll call in the evenings, only to turn up days later having tagged along behind another unit. On 5 September, the date on which the retreat ended, some 20,000 men of the BEF were absent from their original units, of which a large proportion re-joined later.

FOLLOWING THE RETREAT

During our preparation and research for this volume of *Battle Lines* we based ourselves in Noyon which serves as a useful base. The town lies an hour south of Guise on the River Oise and boasts the magnificent cathedral of **Notre-Dame de Noyon** where the first Holy Roman Emperor, Charlemagne, was crowned in 768. The town is only 45 minutes from **Néry** and slightly less than an hour from Villers-Cotterêts. Just outside the town is the 2-star **Ibis Budget Hôtel** which gives good value but if you are looking a little more up-market, the 3-star **Hôtel le Cèdre** near the cathedral offers a secure car park. Camping in the area is plentiful but we can recommend **Camping La Montagne** at Chirry-Ourscamp which can be found approximately 5km southwest of Noyon. The site is open all year round, has a pool and mobile homes for rent. We can also recommend the **Water Mill** on the Rue Gérard de Séroux at Béthisy Saint-Martin which is a few miles northeast of Néry and is set in a delightful location on the River l'Automne.

A good final overnight base towards the end of the retreat route can be found at **Essômes-sur-Marne**, 20 minutes from Château-Thierry on the River Marne. Here the 3-star **Ibis Château-Thierry** with its own restaurant and river terrace is pleasantly comfortable. A cheaper alternative is the **Hôtel Campanile** located in Château-Thierry itself.

Regular visitors to the battlefields will be familiar with the collections of old shells and other explosive material, often placed at the roadside by farmers. This lethal harvest is less likely to be observed over the course of the retreat from Mons except perhaps at Le Cateau. However, there are still occasions when you may chance to come across unexploded devices of 1914–18 vintage or even ammunition remaining from the Second World War. The rule is quite simple – by all means look and take photographs but please do not touch. It goes without saying that walkers and cyclists should come to Belgium and France properly

The cathedral of Notre-Dame de Noyon.

equipped to enjoy their activity. The weather is often unpredictable and it is always advisable to walk in a decent pair of boots and carry a set of waterproofs with you.

USING THIS GUIDEBOOK

As we did with *The Retreat From Mons – North* – the companion volume to this book – we have divided this guide into four stages, with each stage providing a context in which the events described took place, visits to the chief points of interest and one or two detailed routes which can be either, walked, biked or completed by car. Although this means that the route taken by Sir Douglas Haig's I Corps will, on occasion, merge with that of the route of Sir Horace Smith-Dorrien's II Corps, it does allow us to direct the battlefield tourist to the principal events of the retreat and offers a choice of selecting specific rearguard actions. Where possible we have consulted the relevant German regimental histories in order to obtain a more balanced view of specific actions and in doing so have abbreviated Infantry Regiment and Reserve Infantry Regiment to IR and RIR. Thus Infantry Regiment No. 72 becomes IR 72 and Reserve Infantry Regiment No. 165 becomes RIR 165. As each German regiment had three battalions, the number of a specific battalion is added before the regimental number, thus the 2nd Battalion of Reserve Infantry Regiment No. 165 becomes II/RIR 165. A similar abbreviation – FAR – is used for the German Field Artillery Regiment. British battalions and units have also been abbreviated, for example – the 1st Battalion East Lancashire Regiment becoming 1/East Lancashire.

The visitor to the retreat battlefields and cemeteries in this guide will immediately notice the impact of the battles of 1918 and the enormous casualties incurred. The vast majority of CWGC and French National Cemeteries visited quite often contain more casualties of the 1918 fighting than any other year of the war, a testament to the high human cost of the fighting that took place during the final months of the war. Inevitably the route of the retreat passes over ground that was fought over between the end of 1914 and November 1918. It is the line of CWGC cemeteries associated with the final year of the war that serves to remind us constantly that the Allied advance, and the German spring offensives that preceded it, made 1918 one of the bloodiest years of the war. Naturally where our route passes cemeteries and memorials not directly connected with the retreat we do refer you to them, typical of these is the Armistice Museum near Rethondes where the 1918 Armistice was signed and the numerous Battle of the Marne memorials south of Villers-Cotterêts.

While we have provided simple route maps for walkers and cyclists, we have not drawn maps for the course of the entire retreat. The route is best supported by the Belgian Nationaal Geografisch Instituut (NGI)

Walking is an excellent way to explore the battlefields.

1:50, 000 Series and the French Institut Géographique National (IGN) 1:100,000 maps which can be purchased at most good tourist offices and online from www.mapsworldwide.com. However, we have used satellite navigation on numerous occasions and found it to be particularly helpful in supporting route finding. For the walker and cyclist, the larger scale Belgian 1:20,000 or French 1:25,000 Series maps can also be bought in Belgium and France or online. We do recommend that you use the relevant large-scale map when out walking or cycling to supplement the maps provided in the guide. To assist you in your choice of route a summary of all eleven routes in the guidebook is provided together with an indication as to their suitability for walkers, cyclists or car tourists. Distances are in km – the first figure in the table – and miles. You will find the circular numeric references in the text of each route correspond directly with those on the relevant map.

No.	Route	Distance	🚶	🚲	🚗
1	Fesmy-le-Sart	7.1km/4.4 miles	✓	✓	
2	Cerizy	8.5km/5.5 miles	✓	✓	
3	The Oise Bridges	25.73km/16.0 miles		✓	✓
4	Néry	3.71km/2.3 miles	✓		
5	Villers- Cotterêts	4.2km/2.6 miles		✓	✓

Stage One
Etreux to Guise

This section of the guide begins at the 1st Division Memorial at the Chapeau Rouge crossroads located 7.8km south of Landrecies on the D934, just north of that road's junction with both the D946 and the D643 (N43). The crossroads mark the beginning of one of the most courageous rearguard actions of the entire course of the retreat. Yet despite its place in British military legend the full facts of the action involving the 2 /Royal Munster Fusiliers (2/Munsters) and 118/Battery RFA are generally confined to a final stand in an orchard at Etreux. In order for the full account of the Munsters' rearguard action to be appreciated, we look in detail at the actions that took place at Fesmy-le-Sart and Bergues-sur-Sambre before moving down to Oisy and the final desperate fight which took place around the orchard, north of the former railway line at Etreux.

After a short visit to the communal cemetery at Etreux we take you to Jerusalem Farm and the memorial at Iron where the 'Iron Eleven' were hidden from the occupying German forces before their discovery and execution at Guise in February 1915. Just south of Guise on the D946, you have the opportunity to visit either one or two of the large French National Cemeteries connected with the Battle of Guise, namely the National Cemetery at Flavigny-le-Petit, where there are British burials, and the Franco-German Cemetery near Colonfay.

The rearguard action at Etreux – 27 August 1914

On 27 August 1914 the route of the retirement of I Corps was due to take it through Etreux towards the high ground south of Guise. The rearguard for the day was the responsibility of **Brigadier General Ivor Maxse**, who, on hearing

Brigadier General Ivor Maxse.

that practically the whole of Haig's Corps was to use the same highway to Guise, realized that the day 'promised to be critical'. I Corps was underway by 4.00am with the 1st Division remaining in a covering position until the 2nd Division had moved off. By 7.00am Maxse had moved his brigade headquarters from **Fesmy** to the canal bridge at **Petit Cambrésis**, where he was visited by his divisional commander, **Major General Samuel Lomax**, who made it clear that it was vital to hold the Fesmy–Wassigny line until the two divisions of I Corps had passed through Etreux. Not only were they passing through, reiterated Lomax, but they were being re-supplied in the town and thus it was essential that this took place unhindered. Accordingly Maxse issued his orders: first to **Lieutenant Colonel Adrian Grant-Duff** of 1/Black Watch and 23/Field Company RE, who were to reconnoitre and prepare a fall-back, rearguard position just north of Etreux, and second to the three rearguard units themselves, consisting of 2/Munsters with the addition of C Squadron 15/Hussars under **Major Frederick Pilkington** and C and D Guns from 118/Battery, XXVI Brigade under the command of **Major Abingdon Bayly**. Commanding the Munsters was **Major Paul Alfred Charrier**, a man fluent in French and very much a Francophile who had joined the battalion in 1890. Known in the regiment as an individualist, the 45-year-old Charrier was easy to spot on the march in his brown tropical-issue pith helmet with its distinctive green and white hackle of Munster, a nostalgic reminder perhaps for those with an eye for the history of the regiment's origins under Clive of India in 1756. Mentioned in despatches in 1901 for service in West Africa, he had gone on to serve with the Imperial Yeomanry during the Boer War.

Major Paul Charrier commanding 2/Royal Munster Fusiliers.

What happened at Etreux

Major Charrier prepared his defensive positions with B and D Companies at the Chapeau Rouge crossroads and A Company less two platoons at Bergues-sur-Sambre. C Company was at Fesmy-le-Sart. Contact with

German forces that morning had begun early in the day. Shortly after dawn 15/Hussars found themselves deployed right across the brigade frontage with a strong detachment at Chapeau Rouge and another with the Munsters at Fesmy. German forces were evidently moving quickly.

As the tail end of the long and weary column of men and equipment passing through the Munsters' lines on their way south, the 1/Coldstream Guards (1/Coldstream) left two of their companies on the left of the main Landrecies road – the present-day D946 – to defend the bridge over the Sambre Canal just north of **Petit Cambrésis**. By 10.00am, with the sky darkening to the north and threatening rain, most of the 15/Hussars patrols had been forced back and thick lines of the German X Corps infantry, many of whom had been brought forward in motor lorries, were advancing across the fields on both flanks. Those German units that had come up against Charrier's entrenched positions had waited until they were in enough strength to penetrate Fesmy, where a counter attack by **Captain Claud Rawlinson** and C Company cleared the village and restored the status quo for the time being. Further north at the Chapeau Rouge crossroads, B and D Companies were engaged in a furious fire fight at close quarters. In the confusion that followed – aided by the rain which was now sheeting down in torrents – the two companies withdrew; D Company down the Bergues road towards Fesmy – D643 (N43) – and B Company towards Oisy along the D946. It was now 1.00pm.

The message from General Maxse – sent out at 12.46pm – ordering all rearguard units to retire, did not reach Charrier at his battalion headquarters at Fesmy. The cyclist carrying those orders came under fire north of Petit Cambrésis and was unable to reach the Munsters. Instead the cyclist delivered them to Major Day who attempted to get through to Charrier on horseback but he too was unsuccessful. The orders did get through, however, to **Captain John Gibbs** and the two 1/Coldstream companies withdrew to the bridge and continued their march south through Etreux. At 3.00pm Charrier was in the process of pulling back towards Oisy when he got word that German cavalry had been seen to the south. It was an ominous sign that the enemy was closing in.

With German infantry reported to be in the wooded area south of Boué, the danger of becoming surrounded must have been absolute.

There was now only one gap in the enveloping mass of German units and that was at Bergues-sur-Sambre. In conference with **Major Pilkington**, Maxse ordered 15/Hussars to attempt a rescue. The 'greater part of the squadron therefore dashed for this gap and a fierce fight now ensued at the outskirts of Bergues'. Pilkington's men attacked with such determination that the Germans were caught a little off guard and in the ensuing melee over 170 men of the Munsters retired under the covering fire of the Hussars. For the vast majority of the remaining men of Charrier's battalion and the gunners of 118/Battery, however, there would be no escape as they moved south to Etreux.

Exploring the Etreux Battlefield

This tour is divided into three parts and begins at the Chapeau Rouge crossroads where B and D Companies of the Munsters were deployed before retiring towards Fesmy and Oisy. Starting at Fesmy you have the opportunity to retrace the route the Munsters and 118/Battery took from the village, crossing the Sambre west of Le Fort Farm to reach the crossroads at Oisy on the D946. Moving south to Etreux the tour concludes with a short walk where the final stand of the battalion took place, taking in the former railway station from where the German infantry of RIR 78 effectively blocked their progress.

The Royal Munster Fusiliers prior to embarkation.

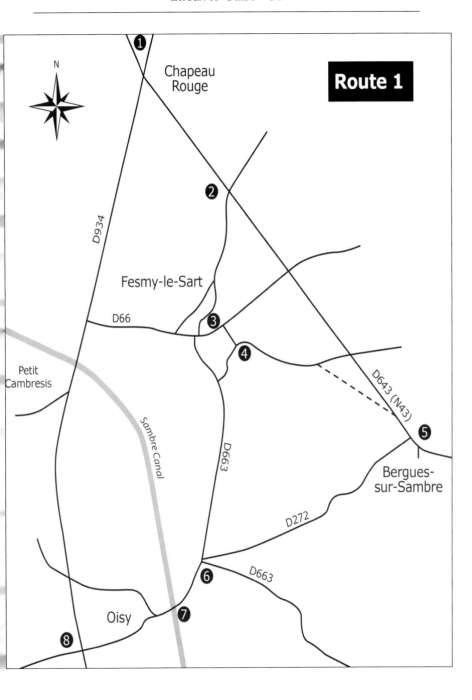

Part 1

The Chapeau Rouge Crossroads

Park in the restaurant car park ❶ and walk across the road to the **1st Division Memorial** on the far side. Take care here as the crossroads can be busy. This rather splendid memorial was designed and sculpted by **Richard Reginald Goulden** in 1926 and inaugurated in the presence of Lieutenant General Sir Arthur Holland, Maréchal Foch and Sir Peter Strickland, who commanded the division from 1916 until the end of the war. Richard Goulden served as a captain with the Royal Engineers in the 1st Division for two years, being mentioned in despatches in April 1916. In August 1977 the memorial was moved by 32/ Engineer Regiment to its present position after being hit several times by passing traffic. The position of the memorial at the crossroads has an affinity with the 'first shot' memorial at **Casteau**, in that it stands on the spot where the division first came under attack in August 1914 and, on 4 November 1918, was the point where the division finally halted on its advance north – seven days before the Armistice was declared.

From the memorial, look up the road to the north towards La Groise. Just beyond the last building on the left, the Munsters' D Company straddled the road over into the fields on the right. Now walk back across to the car park and look northwest up the D634 towards the cluster of industrial buildings to the left of the road. In the far distance is the church tower of the *Nativité de la Sainte Vierge* at Cattilon-sur-Sambre. Between the car park and the buildings **Captain George Simms** and B Company formed an arc across the road into the fields on the left, forming a protective screen against German forces approaching from the northwest. There was fierce fighting here as both companies were engaged by the German advance patrols. **Major Bayly** of the RFA recalled the intensity of the fighting, 'the two RMF machine guns at the crossroads, under Lieutenant Chute, and one eighteen pounder gun

The British 1st Division Memorial at the Chapeau Rouge crossroads north of Etreux.

10 yards behind them were firing heavily on infantry groups at short range, and at an enemy battery in action behind a wood to the north east'. In a heavy downpour of rain and under severe pressure from an increasingly tenacious enemy, both companies withdrew slowly;

B Company down the road towards Oisy and Etreux and D Company along the D643 towards Fesmy-le-Sart. It was approximately 1.00pm. As D Company retired towards Fesmy the two guns of 118/Battery came into action at the crossroads just north of the junction with the D66 at a spot called le Lion d'Or, firing sixty rounds of shrapnel between them. With one platoon from A Company under **Lieutenant Erasmus Gower** as escort to the guns, the Munsters turned right off the main road towards Fesmy ❷ along the D66. Here Major Bayly deployed C Gun which, after firing forty rounds on German infantry formations moving down the road, limbered up and re-joined the main party in the village.

From the Chapeau Rouge crossroads take the D643 – signposted Bergues-sur-Sambre and Boué – towards Fesmy-le-Sart. This is the route along which D Company retired from the crossroads as they made their way towards Fesmy. The first turning on your right – D66 – will take you into the centre of the village. Park near the church in the Place de l'Église ❸.

C Company, Royal Munster Fusiliers, at Aldershot one month before embarking for France. It was these men who delayed the German incursion into Fesmy-le-Sart before the battalion retired to Etreux.

Part 2
Fesmy-le-Sart

Suitable for: 🚶 🚲
Circular route starting at: Fesmy-le-Sart.
Coordinates: 50°02 28.32″ N – 3°40 41.83″ E.
Distance: 7.1km/4.4 miles.
Grade: Easy.
Maps: Blue Series 1:25,000 2707 0 – Landrecies.

General description and context: This route covers the second phase of the Munsters' rearguard action around the villages of Fesmy-le-Sart and Bergues-sur-Sambre. Apart from a very short section of busy road at Bergues, the route uses minor roads and tracks. By the time D Company had re-joined the battalion after its encounter at Chapeau Rouge the Munsters were already in serious trouble. German forces had begun to surround the village and the retirement towards Oisy was carried out within sight of enemy forces who were continually pressing forward.

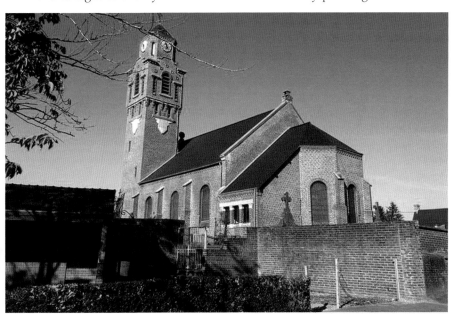

The Church of St Martin at Fesmy-le-Sart.

We have no way of knowing now, of course, but Major Charrier must have been extremely concerned for the welfare of his beloved battalion and grateful for the support provided by the two guns of 118/Battery.

Route description: From the church head south to the junction with the Rue de l'Abbaye and turn left. Continue downhill through the village to the main T-junction with the Rue de la Justice. Turn right and continue to another T-junction and stop❹. On the open ground to the left the 118/Battery D Gun was in action firing some sixteen rounds of shrapnel at German infantry from IR 15 who had penetrated the eastern edge of the village. They were eventually repulsed by **Captain Rawlinson** and the men of C Company, who also took a few prisoners. This was another indication that the Munsters' presence in the village was becoming uncomfortably precarious. At 3.00pm, with no orders appearing from brigade headquarters, Major Charrier ordered the retirement south towards Etreux. Major Bayly deployed 'single guns [which] were brought into action alternately in successive positions to aid the retirement which continued on Oisy'.

Now turn left at the T-junction and follow the road for a little over 800m to find the entrance to a track on the right. Turn right along the track but be warned it can become a little muddy in places after wet weather. The track is tree-lined and rises to join the main road. Turn right – but take care here as the road can be busy – ahead of you is the village of **Bergues-sur-Sambre**. Continue to the village green and war memorial and stop ❺. The village was the scene of a sharp fire fight involving **Captain Woods** and the men of A Company of the Munsters. At 11.00am Woods sent word to Major Charrier that he and his men were hard pressed which resulted in two platoons of C Company under **Captain Emerson** being sent to hold the east end of Fesmy with orders to 'get in touch with Captain Woods'. Whether this took place or not is unclear, but a squadron of 15/Hussars under the command of Major Pilkington were ordered to reinforce A Company and if possible assist them in retiring. Pilkington knew that Fesmy was practically surrounded but his intelligence suggested there was still a gap at Bergues-sur-Sambre which might just allow A Company to get away. It was a gallant action but it was not without cost. In enabling the Munsters to escape relatively unscathed **Private William Wilkes** was killed and **Lance Corporal John Stent** died of his wounds six months later in captivity at Guise. The only officer to fall in the action was **Lieutenant the Hon Edward Charles Hardinge, DSO**, son of the 1st Baron Hardinge of Penshurst, Kent. Hardinge – who was also the godson of Queen Alexandra, the mother of King George V – was wounded in both arms and died of his wounds in England almost four months later on 18 December 1914. He is buried in the churchyard cemetery of Fordcombe St Peter in Penshurst. Tragically his younger brother, 19-year-old Second Lieutenant Henry Hardinge, was killed in May 1915. His name is commemorated on the Ploegsteert Memorial to the Missing south of Ypres in Belgium.

Now find the D272 to Oisy – Rue de Oisy – almost opposite the church. This minor road runs southwest out of the village and provides a good view across to the left of the open ground over which 15/Hussars approached the village. Just after Robizeux Farm the road begins to descend and you can see the village of Oisy ahead of you. Continue to the junction ➏ with the D663 and stop. The D663 to your right is the road from Fesmy along which the Munsters and 118/Battery retired towards Oisy. The withdrawing infantry would have crossed in front of you at this spot and doubled towards Oisy to cross the Sambre Canal before moving through Oisy to reach the crossroads with the D946 to the west of the town. Imagine for a moment the road as it must have been late in the afternoon of 27 August. The long columns of Munsters coming down towards you, the men being kept in line by their NCOs and hurried along by company officers. At the head of the column would have been Major Charrier, complete with pith helmet, his demeanour not betraying his deep concern as to the situation he and his men were facing. Behind the battalion the guns of 118/Battery were coming into action firing shrapnel rounds at the advancing German infantry. At the junction Charrier may have paused slightly as he consulted his map before heading towards the canal bridge and the Oisy crossroads. As the last of Charrier's men reached the junction and headed towards the bridge they would have heard the bark of C Gun of 118/Battery in action in the field to your left, just in front of where Le Fort Farm now stands. After firing ten rounds at the advancing German infantry, which must have been visible to the north, the gunners limbered up and followed the Munsters across the bridge. Should you wish to visit

The bridge over the Sambre at Oisy.

the bridge ❼, it is only another 500m left along the D663 and there is a handy bar on the other side!

We are now going to turn right and return to Fesmy along the D663. There are two short stops to be made on this road as we head back towards Fesmy, both of them at the probable locations of the 118/Battery guns as they came into action behind the Munsters. The first of these positions is at the point where the road bends round to the left, and from where the church at Fesmy should just be in view. D Gun would have been in a good position here to bring fire down on German infantry and Major Bayly's account tells us that D Gun fired twenty rounds – targeting infantry and machine guns that were concealed behind hedges – before limbering up and moving across the canal bridge. The second position was probably 350m further up the road towards the village where the ground rises and there is a clearer view ahead to the north and northwest. C Gun fired ten rounds from here – the enemy must have been very close. You can imagine the two guns leapfrogging down the road towards the canal unlimbering alternately to fire at the advancing enemy and hurriedly moving on to their next position. The gunners would have been working hard to bring their guns into action and undoubtedly **Lieutenant Stewart-Cox** and **Battery Sergeant Major Thomas Strutt** would have had one eye on the expenditure of ammunition. Each ammunition limber only held twenty-four rounds of shrapnel and would need a constant re-supply from the three wagons of the ammunition transport. By the time both guns crossed the bridge they had fired 146 rounds of shrapnel between them since the first engagement at Chapeau Rouge. Continue to the end of the road where you will find the church ❸ and your vehicle directly ahead of you.

> *After returning to your vehicle drive west on the D66 towards the main D946 and turn left towards the road bridge over the Sambre/Oise Canal north of Petit Cambrésis.*

This is where **Brigadier General Ivor Maxse** had his headquarters after moving from Fesmy-le-Sart at 7.00am on the morning of 27 August, and where he was visited by his divisional commander, Major General Lomax. It was from this spot that the orders were issued to the Munsters to act as rearguard.

Continue for a further 2km to the crossroads west of Oisy ❹ and stop where convenient. At 5.30pm the main body of the Munsters was here but without **Captain George Simms** and B Company. Charrier sent runners and cyclists out to find them but it was nearly an hour before they appeared, an hour of inactivity which was to prove fatal for the battalion. Moving through Oisy, Captain Rawlinson's C Company brought up the rear and almost immediately came under attack from *General* **Karl von Plettenberg's 2nd Guard Division**, from which it was only just able to escape thanks to the covering fire from the two platoons under **Lieutenant Deane Drake and Sergeant Foley**. The Germans were close behind and Charrier was unaware that his hour's delay at the crossroads had probably cost him any chance he may have had of escaping the German net.

Now continue down the road towards Etreux.

Karl von Plettenberg.

Part 3

Etreux, The Last Stand

The final part of this route provides an opportunity to stretch the legs touring the area in which the Munsters and 118/Battery fought their final desperate attempt to break through the fast-encroaching German infantry. We have not provided a map for this final phase of the Munsters' rearguard action as the area is contained within a small triangle of ground which can be covered in just over 1km.

As you approach Etreux you will see **Etreux British Cemetery** on the left, marked by two tall conifers behind the distinctive shape of the Celtic cross memorial. Park in one of the spaces provided on either side of the road. We suggest you visit the cemetery – which stands on the ground of what in 1914 was an orchard – after completing the short walking tour. After parking your vehicle, look back up the road towards Oisy. It was from that direction that the Munsters approached Etreux having left Oisy to continue their fighting rearguard action. Imagine rifle and machine-gun fire growing in volume as the rain-sodden Munsters and the two horse-drawn guns and ammunition limbers of 118/Battery under **Major Bayly** gradually move down the road towards you. By 6.00pm the situation was reaching a critical phase. Two German regiments – RIR 73 and RIR 78 – were sweeping towards Etreux from the fields behind the cemetery and the leading troops had already cut the road that runs downhill towards the church behind you.

The imposing Celtic Cross at Etreux Military Cemetery.

As Major Charrier's column reached a point a little way south of the farm buildings you can see some 250m away to the right of the road towards Oisy, the Germans hit it with heavy rifle fire and shell fire from field guns about 1km to the east. Their shooting was extremely accurate. Before Charrier and Major Bayly had time to deploy their men properly the German gunners had found their range. Major Bayly:

> I gave the command 'action left' and though the enemy's fourth shell killed the Sergt., 2 men, and 3 horses of the leading sub section, both guns were got into action on the road 70 yards apart. [Battery Sergeant Major] Strutt lifted Sergt. Perch, who was mortally wounded, from his horse and volunteered to take command of D gun. I ordered him to open fire on a loop-holed house in Etreux about 200 yards distant but all attempts to bring up ammunition to that gun failed, and the detachment was shot down without exception.

Battery Sergeant Major Strutt's gun was positioned some 135m up the road from the cemetery. The gunners had been shot down after firing just two rounds. Bayly's second gun, under **Lieutenant Stewart-Cox**, was a further 60m or so beyond.

Stand by the entrance to the cemetery and look across to the house with the metal gates which lies at right angles to the road on the opposite side. Cross the road and walk to the cottage. This is the 'loop-holed house' mentioned by Major Bayly. Ironically the cottage had been prepared for defence by 23/Field Company of the RE that very morning but now the Germans were taking full advantage of it along with trenches dug earlier by men of 1/Black Watch. The irony would not have been lost on a character like Paul Charrier. The German defence of the cottage would prove to be the final straw in a rearguard action destined to secure a place for his battalion in British military legend.

Major Charrier now divided A and B Companies into two groups to battle his way into and through Etreux on either side of the road. Major Bayly ran up to tell him what he was trying to do with his guns. Charrier's reply was typically upbeat, 'We shall get through all right if you can "boost" those Germans out of these houses with a couple of shells.' It was wishful thinking. As Bayly made his way back towards his last remaining gun 240m or so back up the road, he was hit in the head and knocked unconscious by a shell splinter. At the gun position Lieutenant Stewart-Cox had fired his last round of the fourteen he had left and was also wounded by a bullet through the shoulder. Every one

The 'loopholed' house which effectively prevented the Munsters' progress into Etreux.

of his horses was either killed or wounded. The regimental history of RIR 78 notes that, 'an English battery standing in the open was annihilated by German field artillery. *Leutnant der Reserve* Hempel's platoon of 11 *Kompanie* took one of the guns, which was defended to the last'.

Now bereft of artillery support, Charrier personally led three separate charges against this cottage. **Captain Douglas Wise**, the battalion adjutant, actually got through the gardens and hedges close enough to fire his revolver through a window – perhaps one of the two that are now bricked up – only to be knocked senseless by falling masonry. It was now 7.00pm.

Look back across the road. One of the cottages slightly to the left was ablaze and heavy rifle fire coming from the direction of Etreux signalled that the Munsters were now beyond help. Walk downhill towards the spire of Etreux church and take the first left turn directly opposite the very tall house. The road bears round to the left past a large calvary and becomes a farm track which can be very muddy in wet weather. Continue along the track. You are now walking parallel to the main road and soon the rear of Etreux British Cemetery comes into view across a field to the left. Although Charrier was held up at the loopholed cottage opposite the cemetery, the attack on the left-hand side of the main road initially made progress in spite of several men killed and

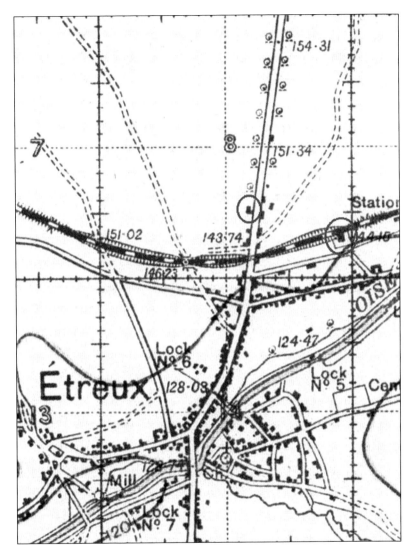

The 'loopholed house' and the railway station (circled) are both clearly marked on this map of Etreux from 1914.

wounded. **Captain George Simms** led the charge of A Company across country, parallel to the main road and towards the orchard – now the site of the cemetery – but was cut down as he reached it. To his left, Boer war veteran **Captain Herbert Swynfen Jervis**, in command of D Company and later to become author of the history of the battalion in the war, had extended the Munsters' line to the east. In spite of the losses, officers and men ran on through the orchard and across the field to your left in a series of short rushes as far as this lane. **Lieutenant Erasmus Gower** was with A Company and had been ordered to, 'push on . . . left of the road (East . . . We pushed on through some orchards and a brickfield to a sunken lane near Etreux railway station – held up there.' Up ahead and to the right you will be able to see a line of willow trees running out across the fields towards what looks like a hedge line. This line is the top of what was the railway embankment. With A Company giving covering fire, **Captain Jervis** urged D Company on across the field to your right towards the railway embankment, in the direction of the distinctive transmitter mast, in an attempt to break the German line and create a gap through which the Munsters could escape. Lieutenant Gower saw what happened next: 'Captains Hall, Barratt, Lieutenants Sullivan, Crozier and self, supported by fire, a charge [made by] Jervis' company. Only Jervis and three men got to the hedge, where [they were] taken prisoner.' In good cover on the top of the bank near Etreux station, the men of III/RIR 78 shot 23-year-old **Lieutenant Charles Phayre** and the men of D Company down like rabbits; imagine their bodies, crumpled like bundles of khaki rags, lying in the field in front of you. It was now 7.15pm and the Germans crept forward to occupy the lane in which you are standing. Yet still the Irishmen fought on, refusing to give in to a force that now completely surrounded and outnumbered them.

Retrace your steps to the main road and turn left. In a few metres you will see the site of the former level crossing. On the far side of the road the last vestiges of the railway track are still visible. The whole area was, in March 2013, available for development and the original rails may not be there in years to come. Continue and take the next turning on the left, the **Rue de la Gare**. You are now walking parallel to the old railway line, the bed of which you can see off to your left, and behind the German firing line which was on top of the banking rising gradually beyond.

Walk on up to the original red-brick station building which you will find on the left, just before the road turns sharp right in front of several industrial buildings. The station is now a private house, but looking across the garden to the railway embankment beyond one can appreciate why the Munsters failed to get across the field as the bank provided such natural cover for the German riflemen. It was in this area that III/RIR 78 bivouacked on the battlefield on the night following the fight. The night was mild so, 'no tents were erected'. Imagine weary but victorious German infantrymen – rifles piled – lying all around, many already sleeping beneath their greatcoats, some chatting quietly in the flickering glow of a burning British rations dump. Their commanding officer, **Major Heegewaldt**, had been shot in the pelvis and severely wounded but casualties for the regiment were relatively light when compared later with those of the Munster Fusiliers. One officer and six men had been killed, five other officers and fourteen men wounded, six missing with two who had been taken prisoner earlier in the day. Retrace your steps back to the British Cemetery and the site of the original orchard.

In the final act of the day in the gathering dusk, **Captain Charles Hall** had ordered the remaining 200 or so Munsters to retire back across the fields to this spot but not before they lost **Captain Phillip Barrett** and **Second Lieutenant James Crozier**. Gower's account again: 'When we got to the orchard I went to report to Major Charrier. I found him by the gun [which was] deserted as all the team of men were killed or wounded. Charrier [was] killed almost while [I was] talking to him, Rawlinson wounded at the same time.' **Lieutenant Moseley**, the scout officer who was assisting Charrier, was also wounded here.

Re-crossing the road to the orchard, Gower and Moseley passed the body of Captain Simms lying dead and reported the death of Charrier to Captain Hall. In Gower's absence 20-year-old **Second Lieutenant Phillip Sullivan** had been mortally wounded and **Francis Chaloner Chute** killed next to his remaining machine gun. A last desperate bayonet charge into the field beyond the back wall of the cemetery in order to push the enemy out of the nearby lane resulted in **Captain Hall** being badly wounded. As the most senior unwounded officer, the burden of command fell on Lieutenant Gower's shoulders. It appears from Gower's account that the remaining men on the right side of the road attempted to break through for a final time at around 8.00pm but were unsuccessful. Lining his command up around the four sides of the orchard – just like a British 'square' on battlefields of old – the remaining Munsters kept the Germans at bay for another hour and 12 minutes as the energetic Gower scampered around encouraging his men until it became obvious that, low on ammunition and with the men's energy

The former railway station building at Etreux, now a private house.

almost spent, further resistance was futile. Gower then took what is probably one of the hardest decisions any soldier has to make: 'Fresh enemy coming up from [the] north so surrendered at 9.12pm – very little ammunition left . . . I could hear no other firing to show any relief coming and was only losing men and doing no good. Also, fresh machine guns [were] getting into position. I surrendered with 3 officers and 256 men'. Around 150 men in smaller parties elsewhere were rounded up afterwards.

By the time of the surrender the Royal Munster Fusiliers had been fighting almost continuously for nearly 12 hours in a rearguard action which had enabled the main body of General Sir Douglas Haig's I Corps to put 19km/12 miles between it and its pursuers. The commander of the German 19 Reserve Division, *General* **von Barfeldt**, later told Gower that the unexpected appearance of the Munsters with artillery at Etreux had caused him to break off his pursuit of the British at 4.00pm and that it had not resumed until 6.00am the following morning. The Munsters' 'last stand' had bought precious time for Douglas Haig's command and many Irishmen had paid for it with their lives. It was said at the time that after the surrender the German soldiers applauded the Munsters' bravery. Surviving accounts do not appear to support this generous plaudit and German sources do not refer to it.

The casualties
The battalion had landed in France with 1,008 officers and men and only 201 were present at a roll call on 29 August 1914; 9 officers and 112 men

were killed, 6 officers and some 130 men wounded with 4 officers and over 400 men taken prisoner. Of 118/Battery RFA, 7 men were killed, 10 officers and men wounded and 21 taken prisoner. A fairly large body of men evaded capture and went into hiding in the local area. Exactly how many is unclear but estimates suggest that between 50 and 120 Munsters were still on the run a week after the battle. Some of these were able to get away with the help of escape organizations such as those planned by Edith Cavell and the Croÿs, while others were harboured by locals but were eventually captured and shot by the Germans in places like Iron a few kilometres to the south. Now enter the cemetery where you will find the last resting place of many of the individuals mentioned in the text.

Lieutenant Harry Newson was one of the Munsters' officers taken prisoner.

Etreux British Cemetery

In March 1921 the family of Lieutenant Frederick Styles bought the orchard at Etreux from the owner, a **Monsieur Charles Dauzet**, for the sum of 500 Francs, and the ground was consecrated seven months later by

Etreux Military Cemetery.

the Dean of Wassigny on 5 October 1921. Among those who attended the ceremony were **Captain Richard Chute** – the brother of the battalion's machine-gun officer – Frederick Styles' two brothers and sister and the father and stepmother of **Second Lieutenant Carol Edward Vere Awdry**. Census returns reveal that Awdry's father was the Revd Vere Awdry who had been vicar of Ampfield in Hampshire. He had re-married in 1909 and by 1914 has started a new family. The Revd Awdry's soldier son would always be part of the legendary last stand of the Munsters at Etreux, but Wilbert, the first son of that new family and thus Lieutenant Awdry's half-brother – who would also become a 'reverend' – would gain even greater fame the world over as the author of the famous Thomas the Tank Engine children's stories. The cemetery is now under the care of the CWGC.

As you enter the cemetery a magnificent Celtic cross stands flanked by two rows of headstones placed along the south and north boundary walls and arranged in alphabetical order. At the rear of the cemetery are the two mass graves where the dead were buried after the battle, while along the rear wall four further headstones are flanked by two stone crosses – on the left commemorating the officers and on the right the NCOs and men. Above the central stone bench is a plaque explaining what took place here on 27 August 1914. There is only one unknown soldier buried here and his headstone lies next to **Private William Wilks** on the rear wall.

Nine of the 2/Munsters' officers are buried here. Among them are **Second Lieutenants Vere Awdry** (II.3), who had been a foundation scholar at Marlborough before being commissioned, **James Crozier** (II.2), who studied medicine for two years before joining the battalion in June 1914, and **Phillip Sulivan** (II.1), who joined the battalion in February 1914 and whose epitaph simply reads 'Died on his 20th birthday'. You will also find the gallant **Lieutenants Challoner Chute** (II.6) and **Charles Phayre** (II.5), whose grandfather was General Sir Robert Phayre. Tragically his brother, Lieutenant Richard Phayre, was killed later in the year at Ypres serving with 2/Yorkshire Regiment. Close by is **Frederick Styles** (II.4), the Special Reservist who was recalled on the outbreak of war, and **Captains Phillip Barrett** (II.7) and **George Simms** (II.8), who are next to their commanding officer, 45-year-old **Major Paul Charrier**.

> *To reach Etreux Communal Cemetery, continue into Etreux until the road crosses the Sambre. Slow right down here as you are going to take the road immediately on your left after crossing the bridge. Be warned, the turning here is very sharp indeed! Follow the road uphill past the church until you reach a crossroads, go straight across and the cemetery is ahead of you on the left. There is plenty of space to park.*

Etreux Communal Cemetery

The CWGC graves are scattered all round the cemetery but the main plot is to your right after entering by the main gate. You will find seven headstones near the wall – one of which is unidentified – all of whom were victims of the rearguard action on 27 August and later died of wounds. Two members of 118/Battery, 22-year-old **Driver James Mortimer** (Grave 44) and **Gunner Francis Shrewing** (Grave 43), rest among four Munster Fusiliers, all of whom would have been buried by the medical staff of the German field *lazarettes* established in the town.

If you return to the main gate and walk towards the other end of the cemetery you should be able to find the solitary headstone of 22-year-old **Private George Lay** (Grave 22), a soldier of 1/Royal Berkshire Regiment who, according to research by Hedley Malloch, was shot by the Germans on 28 April 1915 after being arrested on 18 April. He had been sheltered for a long time by a woman in the nearby village of Hannappes. To the right of George Lay you will find two men of 1/Battalion Gloucestershire Regiment, 37-year-old **Captain Guy Shipway**, who commanded B Company, is buried next to **Private Ernest Smitheram**. Both men were wounded near **Favil** on 25 August and brought to Etreux by 4/Field Ambulance where they died the next day. Guy Shipway was the first officer of the Gloucesters to be killed in the Great War and left a widow, Gladys, and a daughter.

Captain Guy Shipway, the first officer of the Gloucesters to be killed in action.

After leaving the cemetery, retrace your route to the bridge over the Sambre and cross over the D946 to the Hôtel de Ville which you will see directly in front of you. On the building to the left – a school – you will see a memorial plaque which records the destruction of the original

One of the two post-Great War buildings either side of the mairie *in Etreux. Note the plaque in the centre recording that it was destroyed by the Germans and rebuilt by subscription.*

Hôtel de Ville by the Germans in 1915 and the fact that it was reconstructed – in the form of three separate buildings – thanks to a subscription from Les Alpes Maritimes pour le Nord which had been opened by the newspaper *L'Eclaireur* of Nice in April 1915, almost as soon as the destruction of the buildings and execution of George Lay had occurred. The original Hôtel de Ville, which had stood on the same spot flanked by another large building to the north, had been a much grander affair.

Razing prominent buildings was the punishment of choice administered by German *Kommandants* for communities that had sheltered Allied soldiers on the run. On this occasion there is a question mark as to whether it was carried out as a reprisal for the sheltering of George Lay, given that he was hidden in nearby Hannappes, but it is not too much of a stretch to see it as a grand gesture to warn the entire populace of the area surrounding the town of Etreux. If this was the case, it would have served as a grim example to discourage others from similar acts of subterfuge in the future.

> *From Etreux continue south along the D946 for approximately 1km to the crossroads at Jerusalem Farm. Immediately before you take the left turning along the D77 to the village of Iron pull over and stop.*

It was here, at **Jerusalem Farm**, and at **la Maison Rouge**, a little further south, where the remaining batteries of XXVI Brigade RFA came into action as I Corps retired down the D946. The road would have been packed with column after column of infantry and their supply trains. Tired and footsore, the long lines of weary men and horses tramping along would have appeared endless, particularly when you bear in mind that in 1914 each infantry division had over 5,500 horses and took up 24km/15 miles of road and some 2 hours to pass a given point. Four days into the retreat I Corps was definitely in better shape than Smith-Dorrien's II Corps. **Captain Jacques Helbronner**, one of the French staff liaison officers with the Fifth Army, watched the British 1st Division march past him early on the morning of 28 August and noted its 'excellent appearance'. The men were tired and suffering from the extreme heat but marched in perfect order. Later, on his way to see General Smith-Dorrien, he encountered some of the II Corps regiments which, in contrast, 'looked harassed . . . there was some disorder and some units were intermingled'. Hardly surprising given the fighting II Corps had been involved in by that time!

> *Turn left on to the D77 and continue for 600m until you come to a site on which stands part of an agricultural supplies warehouse. Stop here.*

What happened at Iron
It was in this village that the Chalandre and Logez families concealed a number of British soldiers – fugitives from the rearguard actions at Grand Fayt and Etreux – from the Germans. Initially there were nine in number but that increased to eleven in December 1914 after the discovery of two more Irish soldiers hiding nearby. The driving force behind sheltering the eleven men seems to have been the courageous Madame Léonie Logez and until February 1915 the arrangements made for the eleven men worked well. Prompted, however, by sexual jealousy or revenge – or both – the betrayal of the soldiers and their benefactors centred on two of the lovers of a local woman named Blanche Maréchal.

Amongst her many suitors was Clovis Chalandre, the 16-year-old son of Vincent Chalandre, who let slip during one of their assignations that British soldiers were being sheltered by his family. Blanche passed on the information not only to her husband but to her other lovers, including a 66-year-old named Bachelet. Young Clovis was jealous of Bachelet and on the night of 21 February, in a not untypical juvenile response, Clovis threw stones at Bachelet's window. This relatively harmless – if not rather pathetic – fit of teenage jealousy prompted an altogether more devastating reaction from Bachelet. According to the diary of a 13-year-old boy who had been evacuated to the region, Clovis Chalandre refused to pay for the broken pane and so, in a fit of pique and perhaps driven by revenge, the old man drove to Guise the next morning and informed the German authorities of the presence of eleven British soldiers in the village. Vincent Chalandre was arrested with the eleven men on 22 February, and the following day his wife and two of their children – one being Clovis – were also arrested along with Léonie Logez and two of her children – Oscar and Germaine. Both the properties belonging to the two families were burnt to the ground in reprisal. On 25 February 1915 the so-called 'Guise Eleven' were executed in the grounds of Guise Château along with Vincent Chalandre and buried at Guise Communal Cemetery. Due to the execution of Chalandre it is perhaps more fitting to talk of the 'Iron Twelve' rather than the 'Guise Eleven'. The remaining members of the two families were sentenced to terms of imprisonment.

Look over to the left, to the area now hidden from the road by concrete screens. Behind these screens was the site of the former mill. The farm of the Logez family was just to the right of the modern gate to the depot and it ran parallel to the road. Beyond the buildings is the small river – l'Iron – which once provided power for the mill – le Moulin d'Iron – which originally stood here and where at least five and perhaps up to seven of the British soldiers were concealed. The Logez mill was not used for sheltering them after mid-December 1914. Sadly there is now nothing where the Logez farm and mill used to stand. The mill was never rebuilt, owing to lack of funds. Even the River Iron has been diverted from its 1914 course and so it is difficult now to get an understanding of what the place looked like in 1914.

Continue towards the village and after passing several new houses, the red-brick ruins of the former silk weaving factory at which Vincent Chalandre had worked will come up on the left. His house stood back from the road, almost directly opposite. The rest of the soldiers were hidden here and this is where all of them were arrested on 22 February.

Drive on. Ahead you will see the village centre and war memorial. Bear right and park carefully, keeping the memorial on your left.

The Iron Memorial

Stand in front of the monument facing the names of the 'Twelve'. The site of the Chalandre house is about 90m away, diagonally off to your right front. It is marked by a cypress tree which can be seen peeping over the roof of a new house. As it stood back from the road, the former Chalandre house was immediately behind the existing building. Chalandre's house was burned down on 22 February 1915, the same day the soldiers were captured, and never rebuilt. The memorial you are standing in front of lies next to the village war memorial and has only recently been erected after the plight of the eleven British soldiers was highlighted by the Iron Memorial Fund. Following a press campaign and successful appeal for public donations, the memorial was unveiled on the afternoon of 17 September 2011 after a full day of commemorative events to honour the dead and those who helped harbour them at sites and cemeteries in Iron and Guise.

The Iron Memorial – erected in the memory of the men executed by the Germans in 1915 – on the day of its inauguration in September 2011. (Courtesy Hedley Malloch)

> *Drive on and leave the village by the D78 which will return you to the D946 just north of La Maison Rouge crossroads. The road descends and then rises and as you approach **Lesquielles-St-Germain** keep a look-out for the prominent RAF Memorial which will appear on the left by the communal cemetery. There is parking here should you wish to stop.*

The 408 Squadron Memorial

The memorial was erected in 1951 near the site where a four-engined Halifax II aircraft of 408 Squadron crashed in the early hours of 17 April 1943. Attacked and crippled by German fighters after returning from an aborted raid on the Skoda armaments factory at Pilsen, the Canadian pilot, **Flight Sergeant François Roland Pilon**, circled the valley of the Aisne with great difficulty to find a crash site away from the village. His care in trying to avoid civilian casualties did not save him or his crew. There were no survivors. It was through the efforts of Pilon's sister-in-law, Madame Marcelle Pilon, née Dignard, that the memorial, with its distinctive broken propeller, was erected in memory of the five crew members. It is still maintained by the local community

The 408 Squadron Memorial at Lesquielles-St-Germain.

today. The rest of the Halifax crew are buried in the communal cemetery at Liesse-Notre-Dame, 15km northeast of Laon.

Guise

The town is dominated by its chateau which was the home of the Grand Chamberlain of France, **Francis Duke of Guise** (1519–1563). Known principally as the man who defended Metz in 1552 against Charles V the Holy Roman Emperor, he also captured Calais from the English in 1558; a decisive victory that sent the English packing from France and broke Mary Tudor's heart. In February 1563 he was wounded by an assassin and died six days later. Francis's mother was the formidable Mary of Guise and a half-brother to Mary Queen of Scots. During the Great War the town became the German regional military headquarters and it was at the chateau that the British soldiers – the 'Iron Eleven' – were tried, found guilty and executed.

Guise Communal Cemetery

Drive straight on into Guise to the first roundabout. Go straight across and take the first turning left, following signs for Flavigny-le-

Guise Communal Cemetery – the last resting place of the 'Iron Eleven', or the 'Iron Twelve' if one includes the civilian Vincent Chalandre who was also executed and lies in the same cemetery.

Grand, Monceau-sur-Oise, the cemetery and parking. Park outside. After entering the cemetery through the main entrance turn right and then left, the CWGC graves are at the far northeastern end on the right. Here you will find the original 'Iron Eleven' who were buried by the Germans after their execution in the grounds of the chateau. Apart from **Lance Corporal John Stent** of 15/Hussars, who was wounded at Bergues-sur-Sambre on 27 August, the remaining men of the 'Eleven' are all Connaught Rangers and Munster Fusiliers; fugitives of the two rearguard actions that took place at Le Grand Fayt and Etreux respectively. There is one other burial here, **Driver John William Yarnall**, of 47/Battery, 44 Brigade RFA from Seaforth in Lancashire who died of wounds on 25 August 1914. **Vincent Chalandre's** grave is also in this cemetery. Lost and badly neglected for eighty years, it was found and restored with a commemorative plaque by the Iron Memorial Fund in 2011. It is a few metres away from the collective grave of the eleven British soldiers. Chalandre, being a French civilian, never qualified for CWGC care but he has now assumed his rightful place alongside the soldiers he tried to save and in doing so the 'Iron Eleven' have become the 'Iron Twelve'.

The execution site (which served as the original burial plot) at Guise Château has been marked by the Iron Memorial Fund and can be seen provided that visitors make a booking. It is not on the usual waymarked paths laid out for visitors, but staff will show it to pre-arranged bookings after 4.00pm. Contact details can be found on the chateau website: http://www.chateaudeguise.fr/; email: chateaude guise@clubduvieuxmanoir.fr; telephone: 03.23.61.11.76.

On leaving the cemetery – turning right after departing – follow the one-way-system to the main road where you can turn left to return to the roundabout – you will see the tower of the church at the chateau up ahead. At the roundabout turn left to re-join the D946/E44 following signs for Vervin, Laon and St Quentin.

The Battle of Guise
Guise gives its name to the **Battle of Guise** which was fought on 29 August 1914 between General Charles Lanrezac's French Fifth Army and von Bülow's German Second Army. The battle was the French 'Le Cateau' and was unquestionably a French victory in that it

stopped von Bülow in his tracks for 36 hours, broke the solidarity and integrity of the German right hook and, incidentally, put the final nail into the coffin of the Schlieffen Plan. Perhaps more importantly in the long run, it took the pressure off **General Michel-Joseph Maunoury's** Sixth Army enabling Joffre to move Maunoury to a position where he would play a vital part in the coming Battle of the Marne. The French fought well and Charles Lanrezac directed his units with a decisiveness and skill that belied his earlier reluctance to turn and fight. Although the ground they took from von Bülow was only temporary, the sight of Germans being forced to retreat for the first time must have been a tonic in itself for the French, who like the British, had been retreating for the previous week. It was after the Battle of Guise that von Bülow called for help from von Kluck and the German First Army which led to a change in the direction of his advance the next day. Whether this was in response to von Bülow or a manoeuvre von Kluck had been intending to carry out regardless of events at Guise is still debated, but von Kluck's change of direction certainly had far-reaching effects! Not only did it bring him back into contact with the British but it would take him east of Paris and allow the Allied armies to turn the tide of fortune at the **Battle of the Marne**.

The Fifth Army Monument

As you leave Guise along the Rue du Géneral du Gaulle towards Mont-d'Origny you will arrive at the junction where the D946 forks off to the left towards Laon and see the large memorial to the French Fifth Army with its distinctive art deco frieze. Turn left here and park behind the memorial. The monument – also known as the 'Lanrezac Monument'– was inaugurated on 28 April 1929 and is the work of the cubist and avant-garde sculptor brothers Jan and Joel Martel. It commemorates the victory of the French Fifth Army and its commander at the Battle of Guise. The bas relief is highly symbolic, the commanding presence of Lanrezac – squarely in the centre and with map in hand – is surrounded by his senior officers and orchestrates the infantry and artillery to his right and the cavalry to his left against a backdrop of industrial France. To either side, panels record the units that took part in the battle. Nearby there are two large cemeteries which are directly related to this battle. You will see signposts for both

The French Fifth Army Memorial – the 'Lanrezac Monument' – south of Guise.

of them – one the distinctive green of the CWGC – on either side of the road in front of the memorial.

The French (La Désolation) National Cemetery at Flavigny-le-Petit

This cemetery is just 1.7km south of the Guise Memorial and can be found by continuing along the D946. It is situated rather appropriately near the hamlet of **La Désolation**. The cemetery contains the graves of French and German soldiers killed during the Battle of Guise and during the 1918 offensives, together with a number of French colonial troops killed during the May 1940 fighting of the Second World War. The cemetery was begun by the Germans in 1914 and enlarged again after the Armistice. In the centre is a tall German monument in grey stone, and on either side and behind the monument are buried 2,332 German soldiers, of which 911 are in an ossuary. There is also a row of Belgian troops. In front of the monument are two mass graves containing 2,643 French soldiers, of which 1,493 are in two ossuaries. The 47 British graves – including 5 unknowns – are all from the 1918 fighting apart from 20-year-old **Private William Barham** of 3/Coldstream Guards who died of wounds on 26 August 1914. The Coldstream Guardsman may well

Flavigny-le-Petit National Cemetery – La Désolation.

have been a casualty of the fighting around Etreux when the battalion was attacked by German aircraft.

The Franco-German Military Cemetery at Colonfay

This cemetery can be found by taking the left turn on to the D37, 200m or so after leaving la Désolation, then travelling through Audigny to pick up the left turn for the D773 to Colonfay in the centre of Puisieux-et-Clanlieu. The cemetery is just over a kilometre to the east of the village. The area around **Le Sourd** is where General Franchet d'Esperey's I Corps clashed with the German Guard Corps. On the left of the entrance is the French plot which contains 1,333 soldiers, of which 571 are in an ossuary; the graves are marked by stones on the ground rather than the more usual crosses. The German plot is to the right of the entrance and contains a large number of individual monuments commemorating officers of the Guard. A total of 727 German soldiers are buried here, with the other ranks being grouped by battalion and company.

Stage Two
Cerizy to Compiègne

Although by 28 August 1914 significant fatigue and weariness had begun to set in among the retreating British, overall cohesion and discipline was generally maintained by the not inconsiderable efforts of regimental officers and NCOs. By this stage of the Retreat the BEF had suffered very heavily. More artillery pieces had been lost than at any time since the American War of Independence, whole battalions had disappeared in the face of the relentless pursuit by German forces and there appeared to be little end in sight. Despite this, the Retreat continued with II Corps moving through St Quentin towards the Somme crossing at Ham and I Corps marching further to the east.

We begin this stage at Moÿ-de-l'Aisne – 25km southwest of Guise – where 5 Cavalry Brigade fought a rearguard action on the undulating ground northwest of the town. Referred to as the **Affair of Cerizy** in the *Official History of the Great War*, it was, and still is, mulishly referred to as the **Battle of Moÿ** by 12/Lancers. But leaving the question of nomenclature aside, the action was in direct contrast to the debacle at Audregnies. At Cerizy, the British cavalry charge – when it came – was a total surprise and in the 30 seconds it took for 12/Lancers to gallop into the mass of dismounted German cavalrymen after cresting the ridge, there was little time for the enemy to respond. Crucially where mounted action was not possible, the dismounted firing lines were highly effective. The battlefield has changed very little since then and the route we have designed provides the battlefield visitor with an excellent appreciation of the ground over which it was fought.

Stories and battlefield tours of the Retreat from Mons perhaps understandably focus on the actions of the infantry and the cavalry and neglect somewhat the unseen yet vital hard graft, tenacity and courage of the Royal Engineers. We attempt to rectify that with a tour in this stage so from Cerizy we move southeast to Noyon to visit some of the Oise bridges where the Royal Engineers Field Companies worked so hard to prepare and demolish the seemingly endless succession of bridges, relating the events that took place at each site. From Noyon we cross the road bridge at Compiègne where Lieutenant Bernard Young and his section of sappers from 9/Field Company were detailed to demolish the structure before continuing south. Finally, although not part of the Retreat from Mons, we cannot possibly disregard the historic site where the signing of the Armistice on 11 November 1918 took place near Rethondes.

The rearguard action at Cerizy – 28 August 1914

By 28 August the distance between Smith-Dorrien and Haig increased to 24km/15 miles and for the first time since Le Cateau, two columns of German cavalry found the gap between the two corps south of St Quentin. The only British cavalry units available to cover the gap were **Brigadier General Hubert Gough's** 3 Brigade in the west and **Brigadier General Phillip Chetwode's** 5 Brigade in the east. The progress of the most westerly of the German cavalry columns was successfully scuppered by 4/Hussars and the guns of E Battery RHA. The easterly column – led by the **German 2nd Dragoon Guards** – put up more of a fight. Moving down the main St Quentin–La Fère road – the N44 – towards the hamlet of la Guinguette they occupied **La Folie Farm**. A mile further south **Major Foster Swetenham** and C Squadron of the Scots Greys were holding the wood north of la Guinguette with the remaining squadrons of the Greys concealed among the undulating folds in the ground south of the D342 – Moÿ–La Guinguette road. 20/Hussars were on the high ground near Cerizy and in reserve were 12/Lancers, which were at the nearby twelfth-century chateau at Moÿ-de-l'Aisne.

What happened at Cerizy

Launching their attack just after 2.00pm against what they assumed was weak enemy infantry, a strong German force of two squadrons of cavalry galloped straight down the slope towards Major Swetenham's position in the woods at **La Guinguette** with the clear intention of testing the strength of the British positions. The combined fire power of J Battery's guns and the Scots Greys brought the charge to a disorganized standstill and those who were not killed or wounded bravely dismounted and returned fire. Hearing shots from their

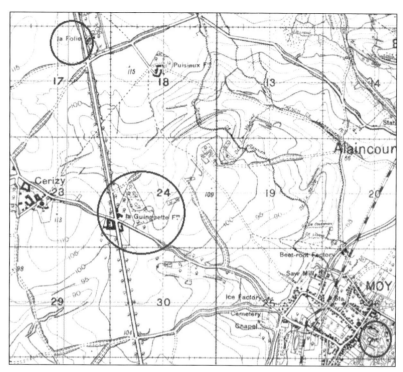

The 1917 French trench map showing la Folie Farm and the wood at la Guinguette crossroads. The position of the former chateau at Moÿ is circled east of the church.

chateau base at Moÿ, 12/Lancers immediately saddled up and joined the Greys in directing fire onto the German cavalrymen who were still on the forward slope of the hill. With the arrival of two further squadrons of Lancers on the Germans' eastern flank a dismounted firing line was quickly established.

The next move was provided by the Lancers, with **Lieutenant Colonel Frank Wormald** directing C Squadron to mount up and charge up the slope towards **Puisieux Farm**. **Lieutenant Harold Charrington** later recalled the moment the squadron topped the rise: 'With a ringing cheer, the squadron charged in perfect line across the fifty yards which now separated them from the enemy, with the Commanding Officer, his Adjutant, the Trumpet Major and two orderlies some twenty yards in front of them'. Finnish-born **Captain John Colloryon Michell** was killed almost immediately his horse went over the ridge, while **Trumpet Major Tompkins** was badly wounded in the thigh and one of Wormald's orderlies was killed, the other unhorsed. The German position, wrote Harold Charrington, was completely overrun 'hardly a man escaped, over 70 killed and wounded being counted on the ground afterwards'. While most of the Germans rose to their feet to fight it out they instinctively knew a bloody encounter was about to take place – dismounted men caught in this manner by charging cavalry armed with swords and lances held no advantage. 'Our lances did great work', wrote **Second Lieutenant John Leche**, 'though they didn't go in as far as one would think – about a foot in most cases'.

Lieutenant Colonel Frank Wormald, 12/Lancers.

As Michell went down at the head of the squadron, Colonel Wormald, using one of the new pattern Wilkinson thrusting swords, was dismayed to see it 'buckle like an S' as it skewered an unfortunate German. **Lieutenant Charles Bryant** had retained the old cutting sword and, well sharpened, it accounted for at least five Germans, 'going in and out like a pat of butter'. As soon as the squadron had ridden through the German position they were rallied by **Lieutenant the Hon Richard Wyndham-Quin** and charged back through the carnage of

The George Wright painting of the charge of 12/Lancers at Moÿ.

dead and dying before being rallied for the last time to dispose of those who still had enough fight in them to stand firm. There were none. Indeed, by the time the two squadrons of the Greys arrived on the scene the men of 12/Lancers had done their job so thoroughly that only unwounded prisoners were left to be rounded up.

In the meantime, B and C Squadrons of 20/Hussars had been sent up the St Quentin road in a bid to get round the western flank of the enemy. As they breasted the rise they came under fire from two guns of the German horse artillery. **Lieutenant Colonel Graham Edwards** immediately decided to attack the guns but fortunately a charge was out of the question as numerous wire fences were seen in the vicinity. In response the three troops of **Captain Cecil Mangles**' C Squadron dismounted some 300m from the German guns and began to put down heavy fire onto the battery, an action that appeared to have the desired effect as much of the battery's fire was then turned upon Mangles and his men who had, at least, achieved their aim of distracting the attention of the German gunners from the main attack to the east. **Lieutenant Sparrow's troop**, which had been directed by Colonel Edwards to cover the right flank, took the opportunity to join in with the main attack and, wrote John Darling the 20/Hussars historian, 'had the satisfaction of getting home with their swords against some dismounted Germans', as did the regiment's French interpreter **'Chirby' Landier**, who 'achieved the ambition of every Frenchman by killing a Bosche'.

As 12/Lancers crested the ridge at the charge, J Battery concentrated its fire on whatever might be behind the dismounted German cavalry. Number 1 Section joined the two guns of 3 Section and together the four 13-pounders lengthened their range to sweep the hollows and copses to the north with shrapnel – fire which 'proved to be very effective against formed general troops . . . throwing them into confusion'. The general troops referred to in the battery war diary were in fact infantry of the **Guard Rifles** who were assembling in a wood near **La Folie**, presumably in preparation for a counter attack which, had it gone ahead, might very well have put a different slant on the day. In recognizing the potential seriousness of this threat, Chetwode acknowledged J Battery's accurate and timely fire on the Guard Rifles in front of the whole 5 Cavalry Brigade at Autreville. Without J Battery's intervention he said, 'things might have gone badly for the brigade'.

Route 2

Cerizy

Suitable for: 🚶 🚴
Circular route starting at: Moÿ-de-l'Aisne.
Coordinates: 49°45 05.09″ N – 3°21 58.08″ E.
Distance: 8.5km/5.5 miles.
Grade: Moderate.
Maps: Blue Series 1:25,000 2609 0 – St Quentin.

General description and context: Apart from the A26 motorway, the ground over which the cavalry battle was fought has changed very little and using a combination of minor roads and tracks we are able to circumnavigate the battlefield completely. The chateau at Moÿ where 12/Lancers were billeted was totally destroyed by 1917 but a memorial is planned to be placed on or near the site of the chateau in 2014. Walkers will find this route undemanding despite the several short ascents in the first half of the route but if you are using a bike we would recommend a suitable off-road machine.

Route description: The route begins in the village of Moÿ where you can park by the church opposite the *Gendarmerie* ❶. You are now quite close to the site of the former chateau. If you look across the road from the church towards the industrial buildings, the ground beyond the trees is where the chateau once stood.

With the church on your right head northwest along the Rue Clemenceau and take the second turning on the right – Rue du Général de Gaulle. Turn left at the top of the road and then right to join the D34. Continue towards the motorway which you can see ahead of you taking the track on the left ❷ just before the road goes under the motorway. You are now running parallel with the line of the A26 motorway which approximately describes the course of the front line prior to 21 March 1918 when the German offensive began in this area. Continue along

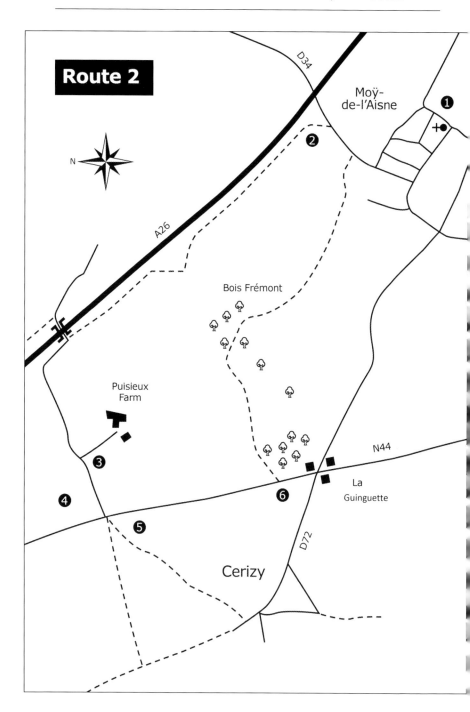

Puisieux Farm.

the track and stop at the top of the first rise. If you turn and look down the track behind you, the village of Moÿ is to the right of the A26 with the village of **Alaincourt** to the left. It was from the direction of Alaincourt that 12/Lancers approached the battlefield after leaving the chateau. Notice the dead ground to your left which clearly masked the approach of the Lancers. Continue up the next rise towards the trees ahead of you where you should be able to see **Puisieux Farm** across to the left front.

The track now skirts a small copse before resuming the line of the A26. Another short ascent provides the first view to the southwest of the hill down which the German Dragoon Guards charged from La **Folie Farm**. If you look ahead to Puisieux Farm you can see the line of the main St Quentin road to the left of the farm buildings. Follow the line of the road down and the wood immediately to the right of the electricity pylon is **La Guinguette Wood**, marked on modern maps as **Bois de Puisieux**. It was in these woods that **Major Foster Swetenham** and C Squadron of the Scots Greys were positioned.

Continue on past the bridge over the A26 and follow the road as it bears round to the left and take the next turning on the left ❸ to Puisieux Farm. Just before the main farm buildings is a small track on the right which runs alongside some private houses, take this track and follow it until it breaks out into open ground after some 80m. Across to your right, where you can see some trees and a large electricity pylon to

The hill leading down towards the wood at la Guinguette (bottom left) from Puisieux Farm (top right). The line of the St Quentin road with vehicles on it can be made out in the distance.

the right of the main St Quentin dual carriageway, is the former site of La Folie Farm. Now look to the line of the St Quentin road and follow it to the south, down to the cluster of houses at the top of the rise at the La Guinguette crossroads. The wood to the left of the crossroads is La Guinguette Wood. The German Dragoons charged down the hill in front of you towards La Guinguette Wood.

Retrace your route back towards the farm, turn left and then left again and head towards the St Quentin road. As you approach the road La Folie Farm was on your right ❹. This is where the German horse artillery was positioned and where the **German Guard Rifles** were assembling prior to counter-attacking. **J Battery RHA** – firing from the far side of the St Quentin road – turned their guns on the farm. It was this action that prevented a German counter attack and in reality sealed the battle in favour of the British cavalry. Cross over the main dual carriageway here with extra special care, remembering to 'look left' first then right on reaching the central reservation. You now have a choice of routes ❺ to take to **Cerizy** which you can see on the skyline. On the left, snaking away ahead of you, is the sunken lane which can be quite muddy after wet weather but should pose few difficulties for walkers. However, cyclists may prefer to use the right-hand path which, although slightly longer, joins the sunken lane just before the village. Whatever route you decide to take the high ground you are about to cross is where 20/Hussars were originally positioned and from where they moved up to attack the German gunners positioned on the ground to your right. Initially **Lieutenant Colonel Edwards** had decided to charge the gunners but the ground favoured a dismounted attack and although the

regiment suffered considerable casualties among its horses, they succeeded in distracting the German gunners from targeting J Battery RHA. With a little imagination you can just make out the mounted men of C Squadron galloping forward to attack the guns and forming a dismounted firing line some 300m from the German battery in what was described as 'a root field'. You can imagine the German gunners heaving and sweating as they turned their guns to deal with this new threat and the whinnies of panic from the dismounted Hussars' horses as they too came under fire.

Turn left at the road and on reaching the outskirts of Cerizy bear left onto the D72 – the Grand Rue – and continue to the crossroads at La Guinguette. Cross the road with care to the other side and turn left to walk up the road for a little over 200m to find a track ❻ on the right heading towards the northerly end of La Guinguette Wood. Turn right along the track and continue for 200m to where the track meets the northerly tip of the wood. Ahead of you is the *Vallée de l'Hôtellerie*. Stop here.

Look up the hill to your left. Imagine the chaos and panic which swept through the German Dragoons as the machine guns and rifles from C squadron of the Scots Greys under cover in the woods on your right carved great swathes through their ranks. **Paul Maze**, a French liaison officer with the cavalry brigade, described the scene after the Greys opened fire: 'The next second the enemy's horses, which were being quickly led to shelter, were stampeding, scampering up the hill, caught in the rapid fire of another of our squadrons'. As the German dragoons bravely returned fire and attempted to scramble back up the hill, C Squadron of 12/Lancers led by **Captain John Michell** appeared from along the valley in front of you and charged up the hill. Paul Maze again:

What followed was timed to perfection like the event at a tattoo, when suddenly, from the corner of the ring, deployed cavalry appears and a charge finishes the tableau. J Battery, lifting its fire, the 12th Lancers who had worked round the right of our troops unobserved, sprang at the scene at full gallop, dashing for the flank of the disorganized Germans. The charge went through them like a flash, and the men pulled up their horses, reformed, and once again rode at the enemy.

Maze was clearly delighted with the outcome and recalls running down 'into the valley as one does towards the scene of an accident. As a few Germans were hiding in the corn-stooks lances and swords were thrust through the hay and I heard fearful yells. The horses were very excited, as were the men, who were showing to each other blood dripping off their sword blades'. For **Jock Crabbe**, a troop leader with C Squadron of the Greys, it was a perfectly straightforward engagement: 'C Squadron Scots Greys took up a firing position and kept the Germans occupied while one squadron 12th Lancers worked round their flank and charged them. Two of our guns helped matters and we picked 68 of them up off the field'.

Ahead of you to the left of the far wood – **Bois Frémont** – the line of the A26 can be seen, and this was the direction from which 12/Lancers approached the valley after first establishing a dismounted firing line.

Continue along the valley towards Bois Frémont and ignoring the first track on the right, follow the track as it bears right through the wood towards Moÿ. Cyclists will be delighted with the long downhill slope which returns them to the D34, while walkers will appreciate the views and relative solitude as the village is approached. Turn right at the D34, then first left, first right and finally left again, to return to the church and your vehicle ❶. If you have judged the time correctly, the nearby *pâtisserie* should still be open for that tempting cafe eclair.

Moÿ Communal Cemetery

The cemetery is a short distance from the church and can be reached by driving back northwest along the Rue Clemenceau and following the road as it bears round to the left. At the junction turn right and then almost immediately left. The cemetery is a few metres further

Moÿ Communal Cemetery.

along the road. After the cavalry battle the wagons of 5/Cavalry Field Ambulance were quickly on the scene with their escort of lancers and under the fire from German carbines recovered the wounded of both sides. In the cemetery you will find **Captain John Michell**, whose headstone bears the epitaph 'He died at the head of his squadron'. **Major Foster Swetenham** was killed early in the engagement, directing fire near the wood at La Guinguette and **Privates Hugh Nolan** and **Charles Coote**, of C Squadron, 12/Lancers, were killed during the charge. Later that day 31-year-old **Trumpet Major Edward Tompkins** died from the wounds to his thigh. 20/Hussars lost only one man, 21-year-old **Lance Corporal William Ryan**, who died from his wounds. The British plot is at the top of the cemetery marked by the flag pole, and next to the 1914 casualties are two aircrew, casualties of November 1943, **Sergeant Frederick Wise** and 23-year-old **Warrant Officer Alan Charlsworth**.

Noyon is approximately 45 minutes southwest of Moÿ and is best approached using the D34, passing through Ly-Fontaine and Gibercourt to reach the junction with the D420. Cross over the bridge, turn right and bear right to access the dual carriageway and head south. This will eventually take you north of Chauny to join the N32 which will take you straight into Noyon.

The French Great War Memorial in the Place de Béziers at Noyon.

Noyon

The town is steeped in history and known for the magnificence of the **Cathedral of Notre-Dame de Noyon**, where the first Holy Roman Emperor, Charlemagne, was crowned in 768. The original Romanesque cathedral was destroyed by fire in 1131 but was soon replaced by the present cathedral, which was constructed between 1145 and 1235, one of the earliest examples of Gothic architecture in France. By the **Treaty of Noyon**, signed on 13 August 1516 between Francis I of France and Emperor Charles V, France abandoned its claims to the Kingdom of Naples and received the Duchy of Milan in recompense. The treaty brought the War of the League of Cambrai to a close. Having been ravaged by Habsburg troops in 1552, Noyon was sold to France in 1559, under the conditions of the **Treaty of Cateau-Cambrésis**. Near the end of the sixteenth century the town fell temporarily under Habsburg control before it was recaptured by Henry IV of France. Noyon was the British GHQ on 26–8 August 1914 and was first entered by the Germans on 1 September. The French were back in possession on 18 March 1917 after the German retirement to the **Hindenburg Line**, but this was short-lived as the German March 1918 offensive returned the town to German occupation until the end of August 1918. Noyon was occupied by the Germans again in the Second World War and on both occasions suffered heavy damage.

By 29 August 1914 the main body of the British II Corps had reached Noyon and was south of the Oise crossings taking advantage of a 'day of rest' from the endless marching of the previous six days. Orders were despatched to the Royal Engineers to prepare and demolish the Oise bridges, a task that none of the sappers were under any illusions about – destroying the seemingly infinite number of bridges was not going to be straightforward. Alongside the Oise – which meanders its way lazily across the landscape – was the Canal Latéral, and each crossing was therefore spanned by two bridges, one across the canal and a second over the river. In some places the gap between the two waterways could be anything up to a mile wide and therefore open to enemy incursion.

Route 3
The Oise Bridges

Suitable for: 🚗 🚲
Circular route starting at: Pont-l'Eveque.
Coordinates: 49°33 42.64″ N – 2°59 29.33″ E.
Distance: 25.7km/16.0 miles.
Grade: Easy.
Maps: Blue Series 1:25,000 2510 0 – Noyon and 25110 – Forêts de Compiègne.

General description and context: This is a route that visits nine of the bridges blown by the Royal Engineers between 29 and 30 August 1914 and is suitable for cyclists and those travelling by car. The majority of the route is along minor roads, apart from the short section of the D934 between the two bridges which can by busy at times. For those of you wishing to stretch your legs there is a delightful 8km/5-mile route beginning at the towpath at Pont-l'Eveque and continuing down the canal to Abbaye d'Ourscamp from where a variety of forest trails and minor roads will return you to your starting point.

Route description: Begin at Pont-l'Eveque bridge ❶ which is southwest of Noyon and easily reached via the D145. The bridge over the Canal Latéral is 200m from the bridge spanning the Oise at Sempigny. Orders for the demolition of the bridges reached 7/Field Company about noon on 29 August and work went on all night while the 4th Division was crossing. A third bridge over the canal – Pont Charlet which was further west of the main road – was prepared by **Lieutenant G N Macready** and blown at 5.30am on 30 August. Shortly after Pont Charlet was blown **Lieutenant Robert Wright**, who was preparing the lattice girder bridge over the canal, had a heart-stopping moment when his electrical exploder failed to work and he had to resort to the emergency safety fuse. That left only the stone

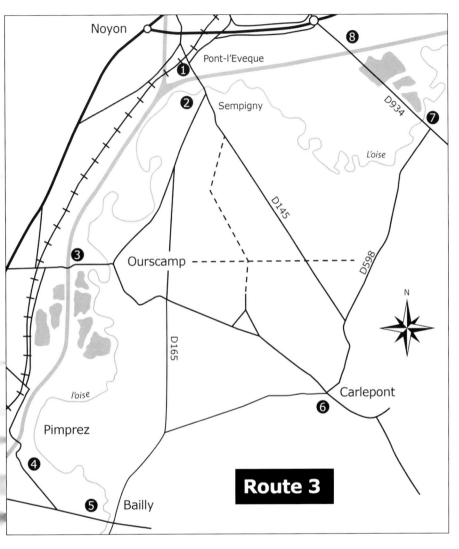

bridge over the Oise ❷, which was being prepared by **Lieutenant Kenneth Gourlay**. The first explosion on the stone bridge seriously damaged one of the arches but did not render it impassable. It was while a second charge was being prepared that the cavalry piquet guarding the bridge was attacked by dismounted German cavalry who had crossed the river unobserved by boat. **Brigadier General Aylmer Haldane**, commanding 10 Infantry Brigade, was present at the bridge and his diary recorded the last moments before Gourlay blew the bridge:

> The engineer officer at the bridge, whose situation was a critical one, hurriedly withdrew his men and ordered the village to be evacuated. Bullets were now falling thickly, and crashing through the windows of the houses, causing the horses of the engineer's tool cart to stampede with that vehicle. But the engineer officer was not to be diverted from his duty . . . and pressed the handle down. The charge exploded instantaneously, blowing a huge gap in the bridge and causing several houses in the village to collapse.

All but two of Gourlay's party escaped courtesy of 9/Lancers which provided some timely equine transport; unfortunately **Sappers Coleman** and **Butler** were wounded and taken prisoner.

Just after crossing the bridge at Sempigny take the right-hand turning – D165 for Ourscamp. Continue through Sempigny passing the communal cemetery on your right. There are no CWGC burials here but often a French national flag is flown denoting the cemetery contains the graves of former French soldiers. The road now takes you through the Forêt Domaniale d'Ourscamp-Carlepont to the ruined thirteenth-century **Abbaye Notre-Dame d'Ourscamp**. Largely destroyed by French revolutionaries in 1792, enough of the basic shell of the Gothic chancel remains today to make it an impressive sight still. In September 1914 the German Army used the habitable buildings on the site as a headquarters. If you have the time the abbey is well worth a visit.

Opposite the entrance to the abbey is the stone bridge which crosses the Oise. It is the first of two bridges, the second crosses the Canal Latéral 600m further west. From all accounts, the officer responsible for blowing the canal bridge was **Lieutenant Charles Fishbourne** of 9/Field Company. Whether he also destroyed this stone bridge is not recorded but the canal bridge was blown on 29 August without difficulty.

Cross over the stone bridge via the D48 – signposted Chiry – and continue towards the larger bridge ❸ over the canal. This is the bridge destroyed by Lieutenant Fishbourne. Cross the second bridge over the canal and proceed slowly now as in less than 400m you are going to take the left turn before the railway bridge – signposted Pimprez – to follow the minor road south which runs alongside the railway track. Having turned left continue for 1.8km to the junction and turn left into the village on to the D608. The one-way system will take you to the first of the two southerly bridges at Pimprez.

Which of the two bridges here was destroyed and by whom is unclear and it is entirely possible that both bridges were left intact. Any apparent failure to carry out the planned demolition of the Oise bridges is mired in the confusion of communication that surrounded the retreat of the 4th Division. Units of the division had begun arriving at Carlepont at 11.00pm on 29 August and the rearguard – **Brigadier General Haldane's** 10 Brigade – was reported to be approaching the bridges at Pimprez and Bailly at 5.00am on 30 August. Orders were sent out to destroy the Ourscamp bridge but for the Pimprez and Bailly bridges to remain intact until Haldane's brigade had crossed the Oise and was clear of Carlepont.

Continue over both the Pimprez bridges ❹ and at the junction with the D40 turn left towards Bailly. The bridge soon comes into view. Cross the bridge ❺ and park off the road a little further up on the right. Take care here as the road can be busy and there in no designated footpath to or from the bridge. There is a tragic story connected with this bridge, one in which orders and counter orders played their part in ultimately creating disorder and considerable confusion. Despite **Captain Francis Westland** being sent out to prepare the bridge for demolition earlier in the day, it remained intact until the final and somewhat last-minute order went out to 9/Field Company – which was by this time at Cuts – for the bridge to be demolished at 5.55pm on 29 August. By then it was already too late. **Lieutenant Charles Fishbourne** started out at 9.00pm in a lorry for Bailly. The promised infantry escort failed to turn up prompting the commanding officer, **Major John Barstow**, to join the party with a couple of sappers in case of trouble. The bridge was no more than 14.5km/9 miles from Cuts but delays in looking for the cavalry escort and some route-finding difficulties through the densely wooded area in the dark meant that they did not arrive until the early hours of 30 August. Leaving the vehicle 2 miles outside Bailly on the Ollencourt road, they moved cautiously on foot towards the bridge. The question as to whether the bridge was in enemy hands or not was answered by a volley of fire at close range. A cavalry patrol, under the

The stone bridge at Ourscamp. There is no record of this bridge being destroyed.

The modern girder bridge at Bailly.

command of *Leutnant* **von Berkheim** of 3/Uhlans from the German Guard Cavalry Division, was in possession of the crossing. **Corporal Edward Sullivan** was sure the German sentry allowed the party to approach the bridge before opening fire; he saw Major Barstow struggling with one of the Germans before running back shouting for the party to take cover. Sullivan was hit by a ricochet in the eye and remembered lying next to a wounded Barstow who was groaning in pain. The remainder of the party – three of them wounded – withdrew at 5.00am leaving a badly wounded Corporal Stone and John Barstow – whom they presumed to be dead – beside the road. Had the bridge been destroyed earlier in

Major John Barstow commanding 9/Field Company RE.

the day by Westland's party it could have been achieved without any trouble or loss of life.

Leave the bridge and bear left – onto the D165 – to pass through the village before taking the right-hand turning on to the D598 to Carlepont at the next junction ❻. This minor road runs through the forest. Route finding through the forest proved taxing for the 4th Division, particularly on 30 August when it took the wrong turning at Carlepont and as **Major Frederick Hicks** of 1/Hampshire Regiment recorded in his diary, 'there was some panic'. Panic turned momentarily to relief when, at 8.30am, the battalion was halted near Tracy-le-Val, Hicks' diary bearing testament to the poor communications that dogged much of the retreat: 'Staff officers kept rushing about saying there was great news – the retirement would cease and the men were to rest. It was intensely hot – we sat by the roadside for six hours, waiting for orders. When they came, they were to continue the retirement'. The language from the men of the Hampshires on receiving this information must have been colourful!

At Carlepont turn left on to the D48 and then immediately right on to the D598 following signs for Pontoise-les-Noyon and La Belle Hourde. At the T-junction with the D145 turn left still following signs for Pontoise-les-Noyon, passing through the hamlet of la Belle Hourde until the road forks. Take the right fork on to the D598 for Pontoise-les-

Noyon until it reaches the junction with the D934 in the village itself. Turn left here and after crossing the bridge over the Oise ❼ stop where convenient.

The destruction of the two bridges over the river and canal along the D934 were the responsibility of 17/Field Company and it wasn't long before **Second Lieutenant Kenneth Godsell** and **Lieutenant Gerald Smyth** were loaded up with explosives to prepare the two bridges. There was little trouble with the bridge over the Canal Latéral ❽ – some 1.6km further northwest from the point at which you are now standing – which was blown at dawn on 30 August as the last of the rearguard crossed the canal. The second bridge over the Oise – where you are now – was a different proposition; Smyth successfully placed his three slabs of guncotton on the main cables of the suspension bridge and waited for the last troops to cross. **Lieutenant 'Papa' Yates** of the Royal Welch Fusiliers remembered sharing his bread and jam with Gerald Smyth shortly before he fired the charges, 'the effect was only partial', he wrote 'and later we heard two sapper officers went back and completed the job'. The 2in round steel cables on either side of the bridge had absorbed the explosion and the bridge remained infuriatingly intact! A second attempt – this time with the few remaining slabs of guncotton – was equally unsuccessful, as was the attempt to set fire to the wooden decking of the bridge. With no further supplies of guncotton, there was no choice left to Smyth but to inform divisional headquarters and leave the bridge intact.

Lieutenant James Pennycuick and 59/Field Company had only just left their bivouac at Varesnes at first light on 30 August when **Lieutenant Roger West**, a motorcycle despatch rider with the Intelligence Corps, arrived with a note for Major Walker to say the Pontoise suspension bridge was still intact. Pennycuick immediately volunteered to go back and see if anything could be done to finish the structure off once and for all. Travelling the 13km/8 miles back to Pontoise on the rather precarious pillion seat of Roger West's motorcycle – with his pockets stuffed with primers and detonators and balancing a box containing fourteen slabs of guncotton on his lap – the two officers arrived at the bridge:

> Climbing up the back anchorage cables proved to be unexpectedly easy. West swarmed up to the top of one of the piers while I was tearing open the box of guncotton. With so solid

a bridge it seemed wisest to put all the available explosive into one charge. The slabs, except for one which we dropped into the river were heaved up and fitted perfectly into the cavity between the cables.

Just as they were about to fire the charge a Frenchman cycled slowly across the bridge. 'We took cover behind a pier and sprang out on him with revolvers cocked. The man, encumbered with a rifle, fell off his bicycle and subsided onto his knees in prayer'. Confiscating the rifle, the unfortunate Frenchman was told to go away as Pennycuick operated the exploder. Unbelievably it failed to work. There was no time to wait the usual 20 minutes before investigating the cause; clambering back up the cables to the top of the bridge the faulty detonator and primer were replaced. This time all went to plan: 'The entire top of the pier was blown away, both main cables on that side were cut, with their ends twisted back over the anchorage. The bridge itself dropped drunkenly down almost to the water, one side of it hanging by a few unbroken ties from the other main cables.'

From the bridge continue towards Noyon passing over the Canal Latéral to the roundabout. Cyclists can turn off left just before the roundabout to take the cycle and pedestrian path that runs parallel to the D1032 and return to Pont-l'Eveque. If you are travelling by car continue straight over the roundabout and take the second turning on the left – Chemin du Marquet – which is marked by the large calvary. Follow this minor road to the junction where you turn left and go under the road bridge to return to Pont-l'Eveque.

Noyon Communal Cemetery
The cemetery – Cimetière Rue de Lille – is a little way northeast of the town centre just a few hundred metres from the cathedral. The main entrance is on the Rue de Lille. The single Commonwealth burial of the 1914–18 war is in the second row, left of the entrance. Spare a moment if you can for 31-year-old **Gunner Rowland Smith** from Kilburn in London, who probably receives very few, if any, visitors. Serving with 48/Battery, he is simply listed as 'died' on 28 August 1914.

Noyon New British Cemetery
Noyon Old British Cemetery was begun by 46/Casualty Clearing Station

The site of the former suspension bridge at Pontoise-les-Noyon.

and 44/Field Ambulance in March 1918, in a wood yard near the railway station. It contained the graves of 144 soldiers from the UK, one American medical officer, two Italian and three French soldiers. All these graves, except those of the French, were removed after the Armistice to the New British Cemetery, which can be found just off the D932 in the direction of Ham. It lies next to the Noyon French National Cemetery and is situated less than a kilometre northwest of the communal cemetery – take the left turn off the D932 just before the two large water towers at the green CWGC sign on to the Avenue d'Alsace Lorraine and follow the road. The British cemetery now contains over 250 Commonwealth burials and of these nearly 100 are unidentified. Another 108 are identified collectively and marked by headstones

Noyon New British Cemetery from the French National Cemetery.

inscribed 'Buried near this spot'. The vast majority of casualties here are a result of the fighting that took place in the area during the German offensive of March 1918, however there are two 1914 casualties, the most notable being 41-year-old **Major John Barstow** (IV.B.5), who was killed at the Bailly bridge on 31 August and whose story we followed above. **Private John William Burrows** (III.G.7) was a 36-year-old reservist from Preston in Lancashire when he was killed on 26 August serving with 1/East Lancashire Regiment. Two 101 Squadron aircrew from 1918 lie close together in Plot IV, **Second Lieutenant Robert Doughty** (IV.D.6), who probably died of wounds on 26 February, and **Lieutenant Alfred Fudge** (IV.D.4), a native of Wandsworth who died on 22 February. Nearby is 19-year-old **Lieutenant George Clapperton** (IV.D.6), who was shot down near Flavy-le-Martel on 7 May 1918 flying a DH9.

Noyon French National Cemetery

Literally 'next door', this cemetery was created in June 1919 and was designated a national cemetery in 1922 when casualties from temporary cemeteries in the area were transferred here. Today it contains 1,022 graves, 2 ossuaries containing 699 unidentified soldiers and 4 graves from the Second World War. There is another French National Cemetery nearby and a short 20-minute journey will take you to the cemetery at **Cuts** situated on the D934. Built in 1922, this large cemetery also contains the graves of Muslim soldiers who fell in the fighting on 5 June 1940.

From Noyon, a 20-minute car journey along the Route Nationale D1032/N32 will take you directly to Compiègne via Chiry-Ourscamps, Ribecourt-Dreslincourt and Thourotte as it follows the line of the Oise to the southwest. Follow signs for Compiègne Centre and park by the road bridge which is near the railway station. Parking can be difficult here on weekdays, but there is often space opposite the Hôtel de Flandre and in the riverside car parks. Alternatively you can park at the railway station and walk down to the bridge.

Compiègne

Nestling on the northeastern fringe of the Forêt Domaniale de Compiègne, the town has a long history of association with French royalty. Used as a summer residence, the forest was a popular royal hunting ground and many of the wide rides were laid out on the orders of Napoleon III. Joan of Arc was captured in the city on 23 May 1430 by the Burgundians before being sold to the English. During the 1914 retreat the British GHQ was lodged at the Palace de Compiègne from 28 to 31 August. In March 1917 it served as General Pétain's headquarters. **Captain Charles Deedes**, who was on the GHQ staff in August 1914, remembered that the 'general situation was by no means bright and the French were in nearly as bad a state as ourselves'. On 20 August General Joffre arrived at the palace to see Sir John French and witnessing this event Deedes could not help comparing Joffre to the Emperor Napoleon: 'Here, at a no less momentous period of history, one was seeing this stout, elderly Republican confronting the same problems and the same enemy which his predecessor had confronted a hundred years before'.

What happened at the Compiègne bridge

On the morning of 30 August 1914 **Brigadier General George Fowke**, Engineering Advisor to GHQ, was told to oversee the blowing of the road bridge. A wire to II Corps requesting a party of engineers with 'the necessary tools and explosives' resulted in **Lieutenant Bernard Young** and his section from 9/Field Company arriving at 6.00pm. Young was staggered by the size of the job confronting him and was much relieved by the presence of another RE officer, **Captain Stewart Newcombe**, who had been put in charge of the preparations by Fowke. Young's first impression – that it looked more like Westminster Bridge – was not short of the mark, the bridge he was looking at was a very solid eighteenth-century stone structure with three arches which initial calculations suggested required a substantial quantity of explosives to destroy it and considerably more than Young had brought with him on the section's tool cart.

With urgent messages sent to the French for explosives – which appeared with remarkable ease by train later in the day – the British sappers managed to find a French territorial officer who produced plans

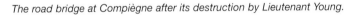

The road bridge at Compiègne after its destruction by Lieutenant Young.

of the bridge and, as luck would have it, revealed the presence of demolition chambers which had been built into the structure. Young calculated that it would still require 400lb of guncotton in each of the two chambers, a task the sappers now began by lowering the charges down to Newcombe who positioned himself in the base of each of the chambers in turn. During the afternoon the French explosives arrived and duly went down each shaft to add weight to the final detonation.

By 2.00am on 31 August the bridge was ready. Young sent his sappers away to rejoin the main column and as soon as the last of the cavalry rearguard was safely across General Fowke gave him the order to fire. Silence! The exploder – which was later found to have a damaged contact – had failed. Young was mortified. Here he was, as he later recounted, a very junior lieutenant with the Chief RE Officer watching his every move at a crucial point in the retreat and his circuit had failed. 'I think all Sapper subalterns will appreciate my feelings at that precise moment when I say nothing happened – just absolutely nothing'. With a quick glance at Newcombe, who was signalling him to strike a match, he lit the standby safety fuse and ran for cover. Half a minute later the two arches that spanned the river vanished in a cloud of dust and fell into the depths of the river:

> I cannot describe the feeling of relief with which I saw the bridge go; if it had failed, I imagine I could have written finis across my future career! Anyhow, I came to, so to speak, conscious that I was holding out my hand to Newcombe and feeling rather an ass. However, Newcombe was made of sterner stuff, and I don't think had any idea that I felt like shaking hands all round, and he very prosaically, seeing my outstretched hand, passed over the key of the ill-fated exploder!

Young, breathing a sigh of relief, put his bicycle into the back of Newcombe's car and headed south.

Very little has changed around the bridge since Young destroyed it in 1914. The **Hôtel de Flandre** still stands on the same site and outside the hotel entrance is the Emmanuel Frémiet statue depicting **Joan of Arc** riding into battle surrounded by eight flag poles in the shape of lances.

The Compiègne road bridge today.

Royallieu French National Cemetery from Compiègne South Communal Cemetery.

Compiègne South Communal Cemetery

This is a large cemetery adjoining the Royallieu French National Cemetery on the Rue Rouget de Lisle and is a 15-minute drive southwest from the bridge on the other side of the river – a sat nav is very useful here! The British graves are in Plots VI and XIV on the northwest side of the centre path. Here you will find seven soldiers who fell in September 1914 and March–April 1918, three of whom are unidentified. **Lieutenant William Ames** of 1/Queen's Own Royal West Kent Regiment was only 23 years old when he was wounded at Crépy-en-Valois on 1 September 1914. Born in Folkstone, he was in command of 11 Platoon, C Company, when he was wounded. Ames died of his wounds on 16 September in one of the local field hospitals. **Private Stanilaus Balfe** from County Westmeath died of wounds on 9 September and 29-year-old **Private Alfred Rogers** died from his wounds three days later on 12 September. Both men were serving with 1/East Lancashire Regiment. All three are to be found in Section 6 on the right of the main avenue. Romford-born **Corporal Harry Gibson**, of B Squadron, 6/Royal Dragoon Guards, died of wounds on 26 March 1918, having served continuously on the Western Front since 16 August 1914. He is buried in Section 14.

Royallieu French National Cemetery

The cemetery can be accessed through the gates on the northeastern wall of the communal cemetery. It was begun in February 1918 by No. 16 French Field Hospital which was based in the barracks at Royallieu. There are now over eighty casualties commemorated on this site and of these, over twenty are unidentified. Special memorials have been erected to five UK soldiers, known or believed to be buried among them. The British and Commonwealth casualties were all brought in from surrounding burial grounds and among these there are eleven identified 1914 burials. There were six casualties of the 4 Guards Brigade rearguard action at Villers-Cotterêts reinterred here, **Corporal Alexander Wallis** (Sp. Mem. 5), **Private Christopher Nobes** (G.IV.62) and **Private Wilfred Bates** (Sp. Mem. 3), who were all serving with 2/Grenadier Guards and died of their wounds shortly afterwards. **Private Michael Dunleavy** (G.IV.61) was serving with the newly formed 1/Irish Guards, while **Privates Harold Boucher**

(G.II.28) and **Frederick Hickling** (G.II.27) were both with 3/Coldstream Guards.

> *The Clairière de l'Armistice – Glade of the Armistice – Museum is situated on the D546 in the Forêt Domaniale de Compiègne, southeast of Choisy-au-Bac. The forest clearing where the museum is located is a 20-minute car journey from the cemetery. It is best approached by taking the N31 east out of the city along the Avenue de l'Armistice – passing the Cimetière du Nord – until the road becomes the D546 after the major roundabout. The museum is clearly signposted off the D546.*

The Clairière de l'Armistice – what happened here

Having spent the previous evening at Rethondes, 2.7km to the southeast, **Maréchal Ferdinand Foch**, his staff and three British officers arrived by train at the railway siding in the forest in Foch's mobile headquarters early on 8 November 1918. A short time later a second train arrived with a delegation from the German government seeking an armistice to end the fighting. Terms were discussed for three days before an agreement was reached sometime between 5.00am and 5.30am on 11 November 1918 when the Armistice document was signed. Apart from Foch, the key people involved were **General Maxime Weygand**, First Sea Lord **Admiral Rosslyn Wemyss**, Deputy First Sea Lord **Rear Admiral George Hope** and **Captain John Marriot**, assistant to the First Sea Lord. The German delegation was led by **Matthias Erzberger** and included **Count Alfred von Oberndorff** from the Foreign Ministry, **Major General Detlof von Winterfelt** and **Captain Ernst Vanselow** of the Imperial German Navy. Just 6 hours later the fighting came to an end.

Initially the railway carriage in which the Armistice was signed was placed in the courtyard of the Invalides in Paris but was eventually refurbished and brought back to the forest clearing on 8 April 1927. At the head of the avenue leading to the memorial site you will see the large monument that was raised through public subscription and dedicated to Alsace Lorraine. The imposing statue of Foch was unveiled ten years later on 26 September 1937 in his presence. In June 1940 the same railway carriage witnessed a humiliating reversal of circumstances when it became the setting for the capitulation of France at the hands of Nazi Germany at the exact spot where Germany had signed the

The Clairière de l'Armistice Museum building containing the replica Armistice railway carriage.

Armistice in 1918. Determined to remove every last vestige of Germany's humiliation on 11 November 1918 which had so consumed him with anger, Hitler ordered the site to be razed and the monuments transported to Germany. The site was not completely restored until 1950. Sadly the original 1918 railway carriage was destroyed by the Allied bombing of Berlin in 1944 but the replacement is a similar carriage of 1913 vintage. A memorial to three local foresters who lost their lives in the war has been placed on the edge of the museum site.

Stage Three

Rethondes to Villers-Cotterêts

By this late phase of the Retreat – towards the end of August – the rigours of almost continual daily marching were taking their toll on the men, **Second Lieutenant Alan Hanbury-Sparrow** of 1/Royal Berkshires noted his own battalion was suffering badly, including the commanding officer, **Lieutenant Colonel M D Graham**:

> The old man is so weary that only his courage gets him along. Behind him creeps the battalion at the slow, lumbering pace of the agricultural labourer. Half the packs are missing, three quarters of the great coats gone . . . whilst not a few got rid of their equipment and carry a rifle and cotton bandolier. Altogether it's a distressing and alarming sight.

But if the British were suffering so were the Germans and none more so than the German 4th Cavalry Division.

We begin this stage at Rethondes where *General* **Otto von Garnier** and the German 4th Cavalry Division crossed the River Aisne on

The bridge at Rethondes crossed by the German 4th Cavalry Division on 31 August 1914.

31 August 1914 en route to **Béthisy-St-Martin**, where he encountered the British 1 Cavalry Brigade bivouacked at **Néry**. Before we visit the Néry battlefield there is an opportunity to stop at the French National Cemetery and the communal cemetery at **Verberie**. The village of Néry is 15 minutes from Verberie and is the venue for a walk around a battlefield that has changed very little over the course of time, and which concludes with a visit to **Néry Communal Cemetery** where a number of the casualties of the action are buried, including the VC winner **Captain Edward Bradbury**.

From Néry we head east along the lovely valley of l'Automne to pause briefly at the site of the rearguard action at **Crépy-en-Valois** and then on to **Haramont** to visit the lone grave of **Lieutenant Colonel Quintin Hogg**, who commanded 4/Hussars in their action at **Taillefontaine**. The final destination is the scene of the rearguard action involving 4 Guards Brigade in the Forêt de Retz to the north of **Villers-Cotterêts**. Here we present the battle lines taken up by the Guards in their costly rearguard action and offer the option of a short walk to the Mangin Memorial.

The background to the 1 September rearguard actions

The first day of September 1914 was one of those days on which the pursuing German forces may very well have dealt a serious blow to the BEF's ability to continue the fight had events dictated a different outcome. On 30 August the gap between Haig's I Corps and Smith-Dorrien's II Corps finally closed and a day later, on 31 August 1914, III Corps came into being under the command of **Major General William Pulteney**. III Corps comprised the 4th Division and the independent 19 Infantry Brigade, which was later temporarily absorbed into the 6th Division when the latter landed in France on 10 September. Marching west, Pulteney's III Corps moved down the western bank of the Oise and reached the neighbourhood of Verberie late that night. Haig and I Corps crossed the Aisne at Soissons – 5 and 23/Field Companies blowing the bridges behind them.

II Corps halted for the night at Croyolles, southwest of Villers-Cotterêts and at Crépy-en-Valois. Looking at the map the astute observer will quite quickly recognize that there were considerable gaps between the five infantry divisions of the BEF, gaps through which large bodies of Germans could pass unnoticed. The source of the problem lay almost entirely with GHQ's Operational Order Number 12 which failed to establish the boundaries of the areas each formation was to be responsible for and left it up to the individual corps commander to decide how much of the area allocated to them would be used. 'To the rather amateur wording of this particular order' wrote the 11/Hussars' historian, 'much of what happened on 1st September can be directly traced.' It is through one of these 'gaps' that von Garnier stumbled across 1 Cavalry Brigade at Néry.

> *There are numerous routes through the Forest of Compiègne which lead eventually to Béthisy-St-Martin – 16km as the crow flies on the other side of the forest to the southwest – and on to Néry, but exactly which route von Garnier and his cavalry division used is not clear. However, if you wish to travel through the forest, the IGN 1:25,000 Forêt de Compiègne map will be useful. But before you cross the River Aisne at Rethondes you may want to visit the tiny chapel where Foch and Weygand spent the night prior to arriving at the Clairière de l'Armistice. Otherwise you can take the easier option and drive around the western fringe of the forest on the D932A via Lacroix-St-Ouen and Verberie – where some of the British dead of the Néry fighting on 1 September 1914 are commemorated (see 'The casualties of Néry' below) – to reach Néry itself.*

The action at Néry – 1 September 1914
On the evening of 31 August, after a day spent reconnoitring the west bank of the Oise for signs of enemy cavalry, the British 1 Cavalry Brigade trotted into Sarron expecting to find billets for the night. Instead they found a French cavalry brigade had beaten them to it giving them little choice but to re-cross the Oise at Verberie, where the 4th Division had its overnight headquarters. At Verberie **Brigadier General Charles Briggs** was informed that Néry – although in the II Corps overnight billeting area – had not been occupied by any of Smith-Dorrien's units and could be used by his brigade. In fact II Corps was not

Brigadier General Charles Briggs.

using any of the villages west of Crépy-en-Valois, the significance of which was apparently not fully appreciated either by Briggs or General Snow. Charles Briggs, although satisfied there were no German troops west of the Oise, was now heading for a village that lay in an extensive and undefended gap between the 4th Division and II Corps at Crépy-en-Valois to the southeast.

Late in the afternoon of 31 August, *General* **Georg von der Marwitz** and the German II Cavalry Corps was at **Offemont**, on the eastern edge of the Forêt de Laigue, where he received word from First Army intelligence that pointed towards the presence of BEF columns near Soissons and Crépy-en-Valois. For the cavalry general it was an opportunity not to be missed; if he turned his units south and marched overnight he knew he could be in contact with the British early the following day. Having received orders from von der Marwitz to march south, von Garnier must have instantly regretted his earlier decision to leave the German 4th Cavalry Divisional transport and ammunition column at Longueil – anticipating it would catch up later that evening. It was a decision he would regret the next day. Von Garnier had expected an overnight halt at Offemont but the news that the division was to undertake a night march south almost immediately meant its units

Georg von der Marwitz.

Otto von Garnier.

would be even further separated from their ammunition and supplies. That night von Garnier's division crossed the Aisne at **Rethondes** and continued through the darkness of the **Forêt de Compiègne**, setting a brutal pace that saw many of his men falling asleep in the saddle. As dawn was breaking, the small village of **Béthisy-St-Martin** hove into view through the dense early morning mist. They were some 3km from Néry.

What happened at Néry

11/Hussars had been acting as the advance guard for the British 1 Cavalry Brigade on 31 August. Having placed outposts around the village of Néry to cover the arrival of 5/Dragoon Guards and 2/Dragoon Guards (Queen's Bays), they moved to the east side of the village and billeted in the large enclosed farm next to the church. L Battery RHA was the last unit to arrive and was allocated the large triangular-shaped field between the village and the sugar factory along the minor road that ran to Rully. 5/Dragoon Guards were allocated the north end of the village and the Queen's Bays meanwhile had drawn up around the village crossroads, close to the field occupied by L Battery and a short distance from brigade headquarters located in a farmhouse on the Rue de Peupliers.

At first light on 1 September the dense mist that had greeted von Garnier's men at Béthisy-St-Martin also cloaked the village of Néry, and delayed the departure of the British from the village. **Second Lieutenant George Tailby** of 11/Hussars had been instructed to reconnoitre the high ground to the east and south east of the village for any signs of enemy movement to the north. On account of his inexperience his squadron commander, **Captain John Halliday**, had carefully selected five men from B Squadron to accompany the young officer on his first ever patrol:

Second Lieutenant George Tailby.

> I took the quickest route out of the village towards the plateau and leaving the main road, stuck off in a north easterly direction

down a track in the direction of the ridge, crossed the little brook and almost immediately found the steep slopes of the plateau facing me. It was too steep to ride straight up . . . when on the top I found the fog as dense as ever and decided to look round the edge of the plateau.

Tailby's patrol had almost completed a circuit of the plateau without coming across any hostile forces when there was a slight shifting of the fog: 'I perceived, at about 150 yards distance to the east, a column of cavalry. By their appearance of their long cloaks and spiked helmets, I knew they could be none other than the much-heard-of Uhlans. They did not see us, however, for they were dismounted, in sections, and appeared to have lost their bearings'. At that moment one of his men fired at the enemy and all hell broke loose. With a slight advantage gained as the Germans mounted up and wheeled about, Tailby's patrol managed to find and then began to descend a steep track down the eastern edge of the plateau hotly pursued by the German cavalrymen. Surviving a fall on the steep slope to Vaucelles, a German cavalryman's cloak and a Mauser carbine were picked up by Tailby as proof of the German presence.'No doubt [the Germans] heard us gallop down the hill and went off in a hurry . . . I picked up the cloak and galloped on', he recounted. Back at Néry, having listened to Tailby's report, **Lieutenant Colonel Tommy Pitman** dismissed it as nonsense, 'A fog is no excuse for seeing spooks, return to your patrol immediately', was Pitman's reply, 'If you saw anyone it could have only been French cavalry.' It was an observation refuted by the production of the grey-green German cavalry cloak and an almost simultaneous German bombardment, which began exactly at 5.40am and came as a complete surprise to the British. **Brigadier General Charles Briggs** immediately sent out two motorcycle despatch riders to the nearest British units asking for assistance before leaving for 11/Hussars' lines with his Brigade Major, **John Cawley**.

Von Garnier's plan of attack was quite simple. Once he had heard from his patrols that an unsuspecting British force lay ahead of him he decided to attack at once to capitalize on the element of surprise. He positioned eight of the twelve guns of FAR 3 with additional machine guns on the plateau facing the eastern end of the village across the valley and one battery of four guns to the south bringing a devastating enfilading fire down on the British lines. Under the cover of this fire he then launched a mounted attack on Néry from the north and southeast. On paper it looked very much as if the battle was over almost before it had begun.

Although Briggs had some idea of the composition of the forces confronting him, initially he had little idea he was up against an entire German cavalry division. In the small field near the village crossroads the effect of the German bombardment on the L Battery lines was catastrophic and the story of the courage and gallantry displayed by the officers and men of L Battery has been firmly written into British Army legend. Fortunately Charles Briggs' professionalism enabled him to rise to the situation. Placing Lieutenant Colonel Pitman's C Squadron in reserve and ordering the remaining 11/Hussars to extend their frontage to include the northern aspect of the village, he gave **Lieutenant Colonel George Ansell**, commanding 5/Dragoons, a free hand to deploy against the German right flank.

Meanwhile, the two machine guns of the Queen's Bays under the command of **Lieutenant Algernon 'Archie' Lamb** had been putting down a very effective fire on the enemy gunners from their position near L Battery. They were also able to target the advancing German columns from von Garnier's 17th Cavalry Brigade, which were attempting to encircle the southern end of the village. As a result of this flank attack dismounted German cavalrymen from the 18th Dragoons did manage to occupy some of the outlying buildings near the sugar factory. The Bays managed to stem any further advance temporarily in a sharp counter attack but they were eventually pushed back as the German dragoons finally secured the sugar factory building. This was the furthest advance into the British positions any units of von Garnier's division made during the whole encounter.

The motorcyclist sent by Briggs to St Vaast-de-Longmont took 20 minutes to make the short 3-mile journey. The reaction was swift and assistance soon arrived along with the guns of I Battery RHA, which were deployed on the Roman Road to the south of the village. The battery had arrived at a fortuitous moment – still in possession of the sugar factory, two machine guns had been brought up by the German 18th Dragoons and were about to bring fire to bear on Lieutenant Lamb's guns – but ranging on the tall chimney of the factory, I Battery put an end to any further threat from that direction.

It was now too late for von Garnier to make the most of the situation, for as the mist lifted he could see British reinforcements were arriving and he was aware that ammunition was running very low. The decision taken on 31 August to proceed ahead of his ammunition column had left the division at a distinct disadvantage – the German cavalry commander had no choice but to withdraw. As a result of its defeat at Néry the German 4th Cavalry Division was unable fully to take up its position on von Kluck's open right flank and as a consequence was unable to provide early intelligence of the whereabouts of Maunoury's Sixth Army prior to the Battle of the Marne. However, despite the limited cavalry screen from von Garnier's mounted troops, Maunoury's advance north of Meaux was compromised by his own poor cavalry reconnaissance. Early on 5 September he unexpectedly blundered into von Gronau's IV Reserve Corps, which was protecting von Kluck's flank, and the element of surprise that had been hoped for was dashed. Whether the German failure at the Battle of the Marne was in some part due to a depleted German 4th Cavalry Division failing to detect the presence of Maunoury's Sixth Army is, in the opinion of the authors, debatable.

Route 4

Néry

Suitable for: 👤
Circular route starting at: Néry Communal Cemetery.
Coordinates: 49°17 04.02″ N – 2°56 33.92″ E.
Distance: 3.7km /2.2 miles.
Grade: Moderate.
Maps: Blue Series 1:25,000 24 12 OT – Forêts de Chantilly.

General description and context: Néry stands on the western edge of a deep valley chiselled out by the River Douye as it flows north into the larger Automne valley. The valley – which is usually dry in the summer – is a wide, flat-bottomed feature that is at its steepest on the eastern side as it climbs up again to the high ground of Le Mont Bethizoy. The village was much smaller in 1914 but today remains essentially as it was on that fateful first day of September 1914, but visitors will find no restaurant facilities or shops. Our route visits most of the salient features of the battlefield and gives plenty of opportunity to view the terrain from both the German and British viewpoints. Although best completed on foot – the climbs down and out of the valley are steep in places and unsuitable for occasional cyclists – the more hardened mountain bikers will relish the undulating nature of the terrain.

Route description: Leave your vehicle at the cemetery ❶, and walk back towards the junction and left turn – Rue du Chaffour – down towards the triangular-shaped grass island ahead of you. As you walk down the street notice house No. 14 on the left which housed the officers of 5/Dragoon Guards on the night of 31 August 1914. The NCOs and men were in the fields behind the house near the cemetery. As the alarm was raised in the Dragoons' lines C Squadron and the machine-gun section was ordered to barricade this end of the village and occupy the houses. Almost certainly 14 Rue du Chaffour was one of those houses as it was then a farmhouse at the northern edge of the village. At the junction turn right in the direction of the church spire. As you reach the square with the church ❷ on the left you will see a large walled farm ahead of you – **La Ferme Roulon** – which is where 11/Hussars were billeted on their arrival in the village. Keep the church on your left and, avoiding the obvious steep pathway in front of you, walk round behind the church to the edge of the valley and stop. This is the valley of the **River Douye**, which in 1914 was devoid of trees and vegetation. At daybreak on the morning of 1 September 1914 the thick mist completely cloaked this steep-sided valley from von Garnier's 4th Cavalry Division and presented a formidable natural obstacle between the German units on the far side of the valley and the British at Néry. At the onset of the battle a troop of the 11/Hussars lined the valley's edge here and another troop was sent to the northeastern corner of the village. **Lieutenant Dermott Kavanagh** commanded the 11/Hussars machine-gun troop and he placed his two machine guns around the church where they were able to fire on the German 3 Cavalry Brigade on the far side of the valley. If you look across to the left you should be able to see **Béthisy-St-Martin**, which is the direction from which von Garnier's men approached Néry.

Now retrace your route to the steep pathway and descend into the valley alongside the wall of the farm. You will soon meet a larger track running along the edge of the valley where you can turn right and continue to follow the line of the wall. It was this wall that formed part of 11/Hussars' firing line and where C Squadron covered the approaches from across the valley. The second-in-command of the regiment, **Major Rowland Anderson**, had woken that morning with a premonition of some impending doom and had made himself somewhat unpopular by deploying the regiment along its defensive line – a drill that was speedily repeated as Anderson ordered them into their firing positions.

The path will take you towards the southwestern end of the valley and soon breaks out into open ground. As you follow the path round towards the trees on your left you should be able to see the track rising gently ahead of you as it begins to climb up alongside the wall of **Feu Farm** ❸ on the opposite side of the valley. As you climb the slope the farm buildings come into view on your right and the ground begins to open up. This was the route taken by 11/Hussars prior to their final

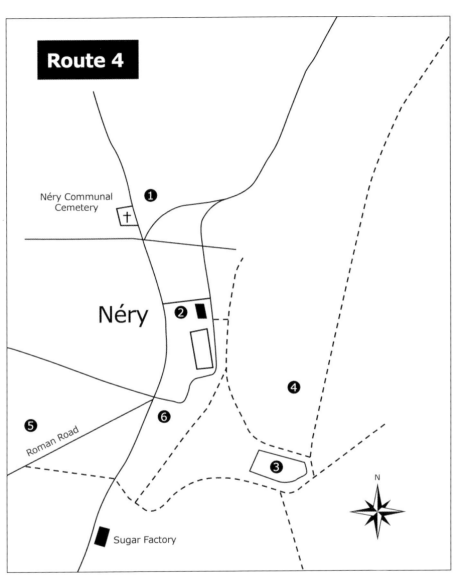

Route 4

Néry Communal Cemetery

❶

Néry

❷

❺

Roman Road

❻

❹

❸

Sugar Factory

N

mounted attack on the gun positions of FAR 3. At the junction of tracks walk into the meadow on the left until you can see the spire of the village church through the trees up ahead ❹. It was in this field that von Garnier deployed most of his artillery and from where his gunners of FAR 3 first opened fire on the village. It was from this spot that one of

Looking across the Valley of the Douye to the Mont Bethizoy plateau.

the first shells fired by the Germans landed in the village and were said to have crashed through the roof of the Meignen farmhouse on the Rue de Peupliers where **Brigadier General Charles Briggs** and his **Brigade Major, John Cawley**, had just received word of the presence of German cavalry from **Lieutenant Colonel Tommy Pitman**. Picking up a time fuse, Briggs saw it was set for 800m and that it was of German origin.

Retrace your steps and return to the track to continue uphill bearing right at the next junction to reach the flat ground ahead. In front of you is the tiny hamlet of Vérines, while over to the left is **Le Plessis-Châtelain**, where von Garnier had his headquarters. Imagine for a moment the scene on this plateau at first light on 1 September; **Second Lieutenant Tailby's** patrol had just stumbled upon the German cavalry column which must have presented a ghostly appearance in the fog. Clearly disorientated for a few moments, the Germans' hesitation handed the advantage to Tailby and his men who turned and galloped back towards Néry. Von Garnier by this time was well aware of the British cavalry presence in the village and had instructed his gunners to deploy accordingly. Once the guns has opened up on their target across the valley and as the fog began to clear, A and B Squadrons of 5/Dragoon Guards led by **Lieutenant Colonel George Ansell** would have appeared from the direction of **St Luce Farm** – from the northeast

– and formed a dismounted firing line. It was during this engagement that George Ansell, who was directing operations from his horse, was killed. The 5/Dragoons attack prevented the German 3 Brigade from attacking the northern edge of Néry as they shot into the lines of led horses. The history of the 9th Regiment of Uhlans records the panic that ensued when the British opened fire and the inability of the German horse holders to prevent many of animals from stampeding. Without their mounts the German cavalrymen were unable to escape.

Continue towards the entrance to Feu Farm, where the track begins to descend to the southeastern end of the valley. Now look across to the left towards **Vérines**, along the line of the track where the German 17th Dragoons had formed a dismounted firing line and a little further on where the remaining batteries of FAR 3 were sited. Descend the track to the junction with the D98 and stop. Across to the left is the former site of the sugar factory which in 1914 would have sported a tall chimney, a little further up the road on the right ❻ is the field in which L Battery had spent the night of 31 September. Close by at the village crossroads were the horse lines of 2/Dragoon Guards (Queen's Bays). As the initial salvoes hit the Bays' horse lines and the L Battery field, horses and men from both units were killed and injured while many of the horses

Feu Farm.

stampeded up the main street into Néry. **Lieutenant Colonel Herbert Wilberforce**, commanding the Bays quickly established a defensive line along the southern boundary of the village. **Lieutenant Archie Lamb** commanded the Bays' machine-gun troop: 'As soon as we realized the direction of the enemy's fire, I collected some of my machine gunners, and brought my guns into action at the south end of the village on the Rully road. We were under heavy artillery fire and rifle fire now until the end of the battle.'

The German attack on this end of the village was carried out by the 17th Cavalry Brigade and was the scene of the final desperate charge by four German cavalry regiments supported by the guns of FAR 3. Thwarted to a great extent by the terrain, the Germans did eventually manage to get into some of the sugar factory outbuildings where a furious fire fight developed between them and a troop of the Bays led by **Lieutenant Champion de Crespigny** and **Lieutenant V H Misa**. Only three men came out of this encounter unwounded, one of which was **Trooper William Clark**:

I was with a party of about fifteen men who were ordered forward, and we reached the sugar factory and stopped a small German advance on that side. The Germans occupied some outbuildings. Lt de Crespigny and Lt Misa led the counter-attack

The former site of the sugar factory.

and Lt Crespigny was killed. Misa, myself and one other man were the only ones to come out unwounded. I was incredibly lucky.

There was a minor cavalry clash in the vicinity of the sugar factory between a squadron of the Composite Household Cavalry and a squadron of the German 18th Dragoons. **Lieutenant Colonel George Ansell** was wounded in the clash, along with five of his men. It was towards the conclusion of the fight around the sugar factory that the Germans apparently used a number of the sugar factory employees as a human screen, although this incident is not mentioned in any of the German accounts.

If you stand by the calvary – *Croix du Ladre* – at the crossroads with your back to the D98, the Roman road on which I Battery was positioned ❺ is at the far end of the sunken lane ahead of you. **Captain Hugh Burnyeat's** four-gun battery of 13-pounders came into action at about 8.00am and were instrumental in sealing the defeat of the German 4th Cavalry Division. When Burnyeat's battery opened up some of the German guns were turned to engage him but fortunately the British guns were positioned close to a derelict cultivator with an upright pole which the German observers mistook for an observation ladder as they put down a very accurate and heavy fire on the pole, leaving Burnyeat's men untouched.

Now continue towards the village up the Rully road, but take care here as there is no footpath. As you walk uphill the triangular-shaped field ❻ which was the site of L Battery RHA's legendary action is on your right. It is hard to imagine the scene of destruction that overtook this peaceful spot on 1 September 1914 as the first shells landed among the battery's guns and horse lines, the chaos, din and carnage of battle must have been horrendous. **Lieutenant Jack Giffard** and **Sergeant Charles Weedon** were extremely fortunate not to have been killed in the opening salvo:

I was trotting a horse down the road and examining his hind fetlock when suddenly a terrific burst of shrapnel and rifle and machine-gun fire was opened onto us at a range of 600 to 800 yards. No-one had the slightest idea of there being any Germans in the vicinity. The horse was killed at the first burst

The last remaining Néry gun on display at the Imperial War Museum, London.

and I and Sgt Weedon dropped into the road and crawled along to one side of the camp.

Sir Martin Farndale in his history of the Royal Regiment of Artillery described the next few moments as the battery recovered from its initial shock and began to deploy:

> At the guns, the left section was watering at the sugar factory as the first shells burst right amongst the massed horses of the rest of the battery. **Captain [Edward] Bradbury** was standing ...with the subalterns [John] Campbell, [Jack] Giffard and [Lionel] Mundy; he shouted, 'Come on, who's for the guns?' The officers and a number of the men raced towards them and began to unlimber B and D sub-sections. They were sorely hampered by the horses tied to the wheels, and the rest plunging terrified, many wounded, as the German shells crashed into the field. Eventually they freed the two guns and turned them to face twelve German guns lining the edge of the high ground some 500 yards away to the east.

Jack Giffard's diary account provides us with another glimpse of the holocaust of fire that was sweeping the battery positions; the fact that the battery managed to bring any guns into action at all says a great deal about the men who manned them:

> We rushed out and got 2 guns into action, myself on one with half a dozen men, and Brad [Captain Edward Bradbury], **John [Campbell]** and **Mundy** & the **Sgt Major [Dorrell]** and **Sgt Nelson** on the other. I had only fired a few rounds when the whole of my gun crew were wiped out, so I went on until I'd finished the ammunition and then got hit through the left leg above the knee by a splinter and peppered in the right arm and back. Then a shell pitched on the gun wheel and smashed it, something getting me on the top of my head. As I could do no good there I crawled back to the stack where some of our wounded were sheltering, they were terribly knocked about. A few minutes later a shrapnel swept along our side of the track, a fragment going clean through my right leg just above the knee and out underneath near the top of my leg, just missing the main artery by 1/8 inch.

Lieutenant Jack Giffard.

Sergeant Major George Dorrell VC was commissioned in March 1915.

Sergeant David Nelson VC was commissioned in November 1914.

Captain Edward Bradbury VC.

In the midst of this tableau of death and destruction the Number 6 gun – Lionel Mundy as section commander, John Campbell in the firing seat, Edward Bradbury as layer and Sergeant Nelson as range setter – kept on firing, while **Gunner Herbert Darbyshire** and **Driver Osborn** kept the gun fed with ammunition. **Sergeant David Nelson's** account describes the last valiant moments of the Number 6 Gun:

Lieutenant Campbell, though already wounded came to our assistance but ere long a German shell burst close to us wounding him and also fatally wounding Lieutenant Mundy and **Corporal [Thomas] Payne**, also wounding me in the right side and slightly in the right leg and piercing my cap. There were now 3 serving the gun, Captain Bradbury, Sergeant Major Dorrell (who up to now had been using a rifle under cover) and myself twice wounded. We still maintained a quick rate of deadly accurate fire until our ammunition supply began to wane and the two men carrying it to us disappeared. Captain Bradbury went to get ammunition from an adjacent wagon but he only got 4 yards from the gun when a shell from the enemy completely cut both his legs off midway between knees and body, thus leaving Sergeant Major Dorrell and myself in action. We fired the two rounds remaining with the gun and with them silenced the only German gun which appeared to be shooting.

This display of supreme effort and dogged devotion to duty to the last resulted in the award of three **Victoria Crosses** to the men of L Battery and of those men – Captain Edward Bradbury, Sergeant Major George Dorrell and Sergeant David Nelson – only George Dorrell survived the war.

At the junction with the D554 stop again. The crossroads and surrounding area were where the Queen's Bays were billeted; A and B Squadrons occupied several houses in the village, while C Squadron were lodged in the open fields opposite the L Battery field. The unmetalled Roman Road which runs southwest from the crossroads can be seen to the right of the private house. On the green ahead of you is the **L Battery and 2/Dragoon Guards Memorial**, while nearby is a more recent addition – 1 September 2012 – in the form of an information panel describing the events that took place.

From the crossroads walk along the Rue de Peupliers to pass Number 41 on the right. This was the farmhouse belonging to the Meignen family where Brigadier General Briggs had his headquarters. At the end of the street you will see the communal cemetery come into view and your vehicle ahead of you.

The Meignen family farmhouse at Néry which became the temporary headquarters of 1 Cavalry Brigade.

The casualties of Néry

The British casualties are buried in four cemeteries over three locations either in Néry itself or within striking distance of the village. One of these is Verberie, 5km to the northwest, while the communal cemetery at Baron lies some 12km south of Néry.

The casualties on both sides were relatively heavy for this early period in the war. During the 3 hours or so the engagement lasted the German 4th Cavalry Division was said to have lost about 180 men – of which 78 were taken prisoner – and they also lost over 200 of their horses. Although they escaped with three of their guns, these were later found abandoned in a wood near **Ermenonville** and were destroyed by 1/Field Squadron on 2 September. Von Garnier's once-proud division was now scattered widely and incapable of further offensive action. The British lost some 390 horses and 41 officers and men killed with another 91 wounded. After the battle about 160 of the wounded from Néry were taken the 12km or so to the village of Baron by 10/ and 12/Field Ambulances and housed in what **Lieutenant Jack Giffard** described as 'a large shooting lodge belonging to a French Baron'. But the next morning – 2 September – the 'hospital' was overrun by the Germans and for the next four or five days the wounded men were technically prisoners of war during which time Jack Giffard's diary noted the death of his friend **Lieutenant Lionel Mundy**. On the morning of Saturday 5 September **Sergeant David Nelson** managed to escape from the hospital grounds and, still wearing his slippers, climbed the perimeter wall and ran into a French cavalry patrol. Help was not far away and before long the advancing French 14th Division was back in charge.

Néry Communal Cemetery

The cemetery can be found beyond the northwestern corner of the village on the road to Fay, opposite the northern end of the Rue de Peupliers. There are sixteen graves of the horse artillery men who fought here on 1 September. A squat special memorial stone records the fact that twelve men of L Battery RHA who fell on 1 September 1914 were

Néry Communal Cemetery. The obelisk commemorating Captain Edward Bradbury VC, Lieutenant John Campbell, Major Stephen Cawley and his brother Captain the Hon Oswald Cawley.

buried in communal graves both here and in Verberie French National Cemetery – seven at Néry and five at Verberie. There is an identical memorial at Verberie. This unusual arrangement was due to the fact that none of the twelve could be identified individually and therefore the names of the men involved are all commemorated at both sites and appear on the registers for both this cemetery and that at Verberie French National Cemetery. On the back wall, next to the headstone of **Captain Edward Bradbury VC,** is a larger pillar commemorating Bradbury, **Lieutenant John Campbell** and **Major Stephen Cawley**, the brigade major. The observant will notice immediately that **Captain the Hon Oswald Cawley** of the Shropshire Yeomanry also rests alongside his brother. Oswald was killed at Merville near Armentières on 22 August 1918 from where he was exhumed and brought to Néry. Clearly his father, Baron Frederick Cawley, exerted enough influence to ensure this unusual departure from the IWGC's standard procedure by that time of burial on the battlefield on which a man was killed, so that the brothers could rest side-by-side. Baron Cawley also lost a third son, **Captain Oswald Cawley**, who was killed at Gallipoli on 23 September 1915 while serving with 6/Manchesters. He is buried at Lancashire Landing Cemetery, Cape Helles. Incorporated into the obelisk is a memorial in stone commemorating the award of the VC to Captain Bradbury, Battery Sergeant Major George Dorrell and Sergeant David Nelson. It is highly likely that **Lieutenant Champion de Crespigny** of the Queen's Bays, who reached the sugar factory and was killed there on 1 September, was also buried here but his body was later exhumed and returned to England according to the wishes of his family – wife Olive Clara Rose, father Baronet Claude Champion de Crespigny and mother Georgiana. The 26-year-old cavalryman's remains were re-interred at St Andrew's Churchyard, Hatfield Peverel, near Maldon in Essex and is an example of one of only a handful of Great War repatriations organized by wealthy families in the days before the institution of the then IWGC Commission halted the practice.

Verberie French National Cemetery

Verberie stands at the southwest corner of the Forêt de Compiègne, some 13km from the centre of Compiègne. The entrance to the cemetery is situated on the Rue des Moulins north of the D123 on the eastern outskirts of the town and contains over 3,000 French

Verberie French National Cemetery.

casualties, of whom a large proportion are unidentified. There are now over seventy 1914–18 war casualties commemorated here, of which more than a quarter are unidentified. The British casualties from 1914 are all victims of the Néry encounter on 1 September. The first of the three Commonwealth plots is situated halfway down the main avenue on the right-hand side. In addition to the six men killed in 1918 who lie here there are five cavalrymen who were killed at Néry, including 42-year-old **Lieutenant Colonel George Ansell**, who commanded 5/Dragoon Guards. The remaining two Commonwealth plots are at the rear of the cemetery. On the left a plot of ten headstones commemorates twenty-seven casualties of 1 September and on the right are thirteen 1918 casualties and two RAF aircrew from 27 Squadron who were shot down on 10 June 1918. Also included are the names of twelve of the seventeen men of the 2nd and 5th Dragoon Guards, who fell at Néry and are buried in this common plot. Note the special memorial stone to the men of L Battery which is identical to that in Néry Communal Cemetery.

Verberie Communal Cemetery

This cemetery is a few metres further northeast along the Rue des Moulins. To find the CWGC plot bear right after entering the cemetery and continue up the steps. The five headstones are on the right. All five are casualties of 1 September 1914 and all were serving with 2/Inniskilling Fusiliers.

Baron Communal Cemetery

About 20 minutes or so south of Néry – via the D113 and the D100 – is the small village of Baron; the last resting place of a further sixteen casualties of the 1914 fighting. The cemetery is on the Rue du Cimetière some 40m north of the church off the D330A. Park in the nearby square and walk round to the cemetery entrance where you will find the two CWGC plots – in effect mass graves – immediately in front of you. Here are a further six members of L Battery RHA and many of the men buried here died of wounds in the temporary hospital. One of these was 28-year-old **Lieutenant Lionel Mundy**, who died of wounds on 3 September. He was commissioned into the RHA in 1906, five years before **Lieutenant Percy Voltelin Heath** was commissioned into the Royal Horse Guards. Heath was the son of Sir James Heath and died of wounds on 4 September. **Lieutenant Lynton White** was attached to 2/Dragoon Guards and died of wounds on 3 September. The son of Sir Woolmer White of Southleigh Park, Havant, he left a widow, Dorothy. Londoner **Sergeant Charles Weedon** was exercising one of the L Battery horses along the Rully road at Néry when the first salvo of the German artillery bombardment fell on the village. He was badly wounded later in the battle and died on 8 September.

From Nery head northeast and return to Béthisy-St-Martin and then take the D123 to drive east along the Automne valley through Orrouy to the junction with the D332 at Gilocourt. Turn right on to the D332 and continue through Béthancourt-en-Valois towards Crépy-en-Valois until you reach the left-hand turning for Morcourt and stop.

The rearguard action at Crépy-en-Valois – 1 September 1914

At Crépy-en-Valois, as happened at Néry, the German advance guard came into contact with the British outpost lines in what must have been another chance encounter. That morning 1/Royal West Kents and

2/Duke of Wellington's were deployed either side of the D332 Crépy road on the high ground north of Crépy with two batteries of XXVII Brigade guns further back on the present-day D335, around the former sugar factory north of the Crépy suburb of Mermont.

What happened at Crépy-en-Valois

The attack developed down the D332 Crépy road – along which you have just travelled. Unable to reply with any counter-battery fire of their own, German troops were at a huge disadvantage and it was **Major Ernest Alexander's** 119/Battery – you may remember it was this battery that fought at Audregnies – which brought the German advance to a standstill with its accurate shellfire. **Captain Josslyn Ramsden** was the XXVII Brigade adjutant:

> At about 4am being again on rearguard with the 13th Infantry Brigade under General Cuthbert, we were ordered to occupy positions at once as a considerable force of Germans were advancing. The colonel, who seems to have an instinct for placing guns in splendid positions, took me forward into the advanced infantry line. We had just stopped to speak to the officer commanding the left section of the infantry line on the Béthancourt–Crépy road about 1½ miles north of Crépy, when [General] Cuthbert's horse was shot under him, the first shot – then the game began. For an hour we sat where we were till it became evident the enemy were in some force – we know now, and surmised then, that they had been sent on in large motors. The colonel now sent me back for 2 guns of the 119th which he had left behind a ridge. Mr Tenison [**Lieutenant William Tenison**] 119th brought up a section and we started firing into the Germans at about 1,400 yards over our own infantry about 100 yards in front! I believe we did great execution with these two guns which fired a marvellous lot of ammunition. Anyhow their fire completely checked the enemy and although we withdrew about noon – battery by battery – to a new position 5 miles further south we were never attacked again.

The advanced infantry line referred to by Captain Josslyn Ramsden was most probably running west–east, a little to the south of the line of the Morcourt road. The 1/Royal West Kents were to the left of the D332 and 2/Duke of Wellington's were on the other side of the road. 2/KOYLI was also turned out to support the right of the firing line and, expecting casualties, the battalion medical officer, **Lieutenant Cyril Helm**, turned a nearby farm into a dressing station: 'Having arranged things to the best of my ability, I strolled off to see how the others were getting on . . . almost at once our guns started firing at a wood about a mile away where cavalry had been seen. The Germans had no horse artillery with them, so could only reply with desultory rifle fire'. The wood – in all probability the wooded area to the south of Morcourt – had been fired upon by **Captain Geoffrey Masters'** section of 119/Battery which discouraged any further advance from that direction for the time being with extremely accurate shrapnel fire.

About this time two motor cars with machine guns were seen driving down the Béthancourt road towards the British lines. The Dukes held their fire until both cars had closed to 150m. Ramsden watched as the Dukes, 'opened fire and shot the driver of the first car, the second went so fast that it ran into the first and was wrecked'. One of the vehicles, wrote Cyril Helm, 'contained four German staff officers – all dead of course – and a good many bottles of looted champagne'. **Lieutenant Henry O'Kelly**, a platoon commander with 2/Duke of Wellington's, described the events which resulted in his award of the DSO in a little more detail:

A little later two motor-cars came spinning down the road towards our trenches. I had the greatest difficulty in keeping the men from firing until they got to close range. Other troops did open fire on them. At about 300 yards we loosed off and succeeded in stopping the motor-cars, which were armoured. Immediately we came under a veritable hail of bullets from the wood . . . We charged out with fixed bayonets and reached the motor-cars right enough. There was an old General potting at me with an automatic pistol, and I determined not to miss him, so, as I am a hopeless shot with a revolver, I shoved it in his face and pulled the trigger, nearly blowing the poor old chap's head off. The men prodded most of the others, and some had already been hit with rifle bullets. I tried to start the cars but could not get either going, so was obliged to leave everything as we were under very heavy fire from the edge of the wood. We first bust up a gun which they had mounted on the rear car. I also took all the dispatches and relieved the old general of his revolver, which I still have, and some good cigars and cigarettes. I also took a few other things, which I afterwards lost.

At 1.00 pm the British began retiring south through Crépy-en-Valois.

Crépy-en-Valois Communal Cemetery

The communal cemetery is on the higher ground just north of the town on the D332 after the road has ascended the slopes of the valley. It contains ten casualties, of which three are unidentified. From the entrance you will see the CWGC headstones across to the right along with two rows of French graves along the walls of the cemetery. The four identified British soldiers from the 1914 rearguard action are from 1/Royal West Kent Regiment and the 2/KOSB, which fought on the high ground nearby. **Private Benjamin Burgon** of B Company 2/KOSB and **Private Frank Perfill** of the Royal West Kents from Welling in Kent,

Crépy-en-Valois Communal Cemetery.

were killed, both aged 19, on 1 September along with **Lance Corporal Frank Bishop**, a 38-year-old regular soldier from Hastings who was also serving with Royal West Kents. Frank Bishop enlisted in 1896 and was promoted to lance corporal in April 1913 having completed seventeen years' continuous service in India, Egypt and England. The remaining 1914 casualty, **Lance Corporal Henry Cain** of the Royal West Kents, died of his wounds on 21 October 1914. **Private James Lee**, 1/8 Scottish Rifles, and **Private George Turner**, 1/7 Cheshires, were killed on 23 and 24 July 1918.

From the cemetery head north along the D332 through Béthancourt-en-Valois to Gilocourt to join the D32 heading east through Elincourt and Vattier Voisin to Pondron, where you can pick up the D50 – which turns into the D80 – to Haramont via Bonneuil-en-Valois and Eméville. Arriving in Haramont the communal cemetery is found by taking the left turn on to the D806 – Route de la Montagne – and after 500m the minor road on the right – Rue de Cimetière – just as the main road begins to run north through the Bois d'Haramont.

Haramont Communal Cemetery

There are only two casualties here and both are to the left of the entrance. **Lieutenant Colonel Ian Graham Hogg** can be found near the wall marked by a non-standard headstone. The 39-year-old soldier was commanding officer of 4/Hussars and was wounded at Taillefontaine on 1 September before he was brought to Haramont, where he died the next day in the school house attended by the regimental doctor. Hogg's father was Quintin Hogg, the philanthropist, Association Football pioneer – he turned out for the famous Wanderers FC – and founder of the Regent Street Polytechnic, which later became part of the London Polytechnic and is now known as the University of Westminster. Like his father before him, Ian Hogg attended Eton before joining the army in 1896. Awarded the DSO for his services with the African Frontier Force, he also served in the Boer War before being appointed to the command of his regiment in 1913. Close by is **Private Reginald Sturt** from Chobham in Surrey, who was killed on 24 July 1918. Tragically his brother, 19-year-old **Private Herbert Sturt**, was killed serving with 12/Manchesters on 6 September 1918.

Lieutenant Colonel Ian Hogg's grave at Haramont Communal Cemetery.

> *Leave the cemetery and return to the D806 then turn right at the junction with the D973 in the direction of* **Villers-Cotterêts**. *Continue for just over a kilometre then turn left at the junction known as the* **Carrefour des Quatre Gardes**. *Drive carefully now towards the Ronde de la Reine as at the time of writing there were a number of deep potholes in the road. After 2.5km you will arrive at the* **Carrefour du Ronde de la Reine** *and the* **Maison Forestière du Ronde de la Reine**.

The rearguard action at Villers-Cotterêts – 1 September 1914

The action in the forest north of Villers-Cotterêts was the third of the major attacks made on the BEF on 1 September. Early on 1 September I Corps was converging on Villers-Cotterêts through the Forêt Domaniale de Retz and the 2nd Division's route took it through **Vivières** to this spot, the Rond de la Reine, a small forest clearing some 5km north of Villers-Cotterêts. 4 Guards Brigade was ordered to provide the rearguard for the division.

What happened in the Forêt de Retz

Expecting a fight, 1/Irish Guards deployed at **Puiseux-en-Retz** on the east of the present-day D811 – the Soucy–Villers-Cotterêts road – while 2/Coldstream Guards extended the line along the edge of the forest to the west of the road, both battalions under the overall command of **Lieutenant Colonel George Morris** of the Irish Guards. Then 2/Grenadier Guards and 3/Coldstream passed through their lines and fell back to a ride running east–west from the Ronde de la Reine. While 6.5km further west, 3 Cavalry Brigade was already engaged with the advanced guard of the German III Corps at **Taillefontaine** on the northwestern edge of the forest. **Lieutenant Colonel Ian Hogg** and 4/Hussars were under attack from cavalry and infantry advancing out of **Roye St Nicholas**, the small village to the north which Colonel Hogg's men had vacated only a few hours earlier. With orders to hold a line in the forest until 12.30pm, A and C Squadrons were gradually pushed back by sheer weight of numbers during which the 39-year-old Colonel Hogg was seriously wounded while directing C Squadron's retirement.

In the meantime the two battalions of Coldstream and Irish Guards were holding their own at **Puiseux-en-Retz** and with the help of

9/Battery RFA were effectively bringing the German advance to a halt. Suspecting that the enemy had been temporarily discouraged from further offensive action, Morris sent word again to **Colonel Cecil Pereira** with instructions for his battalion of 2/Coldstream Guards to fall back to the railway line looping due east from Villers-Cotterêts. Morris was preparing to follow them when he was ordered to stay put as the main body of the division was to halt for their lunches until 1.00pm. The Coldstream were already past recall by this time which left the Irish Guards isolated and extremely vulnerable, and in the considered opinion of one officer, 'if the division took too long over their lunches the Irish Guards would probably be wiped out', a view shared by **Major George Jeffreys** on the Ronde de la Reine with the Grenadiers. Jeffreys' astonishment at the order was only tempered by the arrival of some of Chetwode's 5 Cavalry Brigade, who halted at the Rond de la Reine and dismounted: 'We all had a good many friends amongst the officers, we stood talking together for quite a considerable time, a risky proceeding considering how vulnerable their horses were, and that they were masking our fire should the Germans come on'. The two regiments of cavalry were the Scots Greys and 12/Lancers and they had approached the Ronde de la Reine from the east en route to provide support to the left flank. It was not long after the cavalrymen had left that this peaceful forest ride became the scene of a fierce close-quarters battle.

Route 5

Villers-Cotterêts

Suitable for: 🚕
Circular route starting at: Ronde de la Reine.
Coordinates: 49°17 01.16″ N – 3°06 38.95″ E.
Distance: 4.2km/2.6 miles.
Grade: Moderate.
Maps: Blue Series 1:25,000 25 12 OT – Villers-Cotterêts.

General description and context: This route is divided into two separate locations and visits the Guards Grave Cemetery, the Cecil Memorial and the Mangin Memorial. We first visit the line taken up at dawn on 1 September by 1/Irish Guards and 2/Coldstream Guards and then move to the second position at the Ronde de la Reine where 2/Grenadier Guards and 3/Coldstream Guards held the line of the Route du Faite to allow the Irish Guards to fall back towards Villers-Cotterêts. Although the tour is best covered by vehicle, there is a very attractive 4km/2.5 mile walk from the Ronde de la Reine to the Mangin Memorial along the ride where the Grenadiers were positioned.

Route description: Arriving at the Maison Forestière du Ronde de la Reine, ahead of you is a no-entry board ❶. Take the turning on the right which leads down to the D81 almost opposite the **Guards' Grave Cemetery**. We suggest you visit the cemetery ❷ after the tour returns you to the Maison Forestière. Turn left onto the D81 following the sharp left-hand bend to pass the **Cecil Memorial** on the left by the crossroads. This is the **Ronde de la Reine** ❸ which we will return to later when there will be opportunity to take a closer look at the memorial. Continue along the D81 downhill towards **Vivières** taking the next turning on the right – the D811 – to **Puiseux-en-Retz**. The road descends through the forest to a crossroads ❹ with a small electrical sub-station on the right. To the right the road descends to

The crossroads west of Puiseux where 2/Coldstream Guards deployed on the edge of the forest along the line of the Vivières road.

Puiseux while to the left the D250 heads towards Vivières. Ahead of you the road climbs up to the high ground of *Le Trou Tonnerre* and **Soucy**.

The crossroads is the centre of the position along which the Guards deployed early on 1 September. The majority of the 2nd Division had retired through Vivières on their way south but 4 Guards Brigade had arrived at this point via Soucy and Puiseux. Once the orders to act as rearguard had been passed to **Brigadier General Robert Scott-Kerr**, 2/Coldstream Guards, under the command of **Lieutenant Colonel Cecil Pereira,** deployed along the edge of the forest towards Vivières facing north. The right of the line – towards Puiseux – was the responsibility of 1/Irish Guards and their commanding officer, **Lieutenant Colonel the Hon George Morris**. It was through these two battalions – under the overall command of George Morris – that 2/Grenadier Guards and 3/Coldstream Guards marched before heading south on the D811 – in the opposite direction to that you have just travelled – to reach the Rond de la Reine.

If you drive up the hill towards Soucy to the small agricultural layby on the right ❺, you will be able to see the line of the forest along which Morris deployed his battalion. Picture the men here in the cold light of

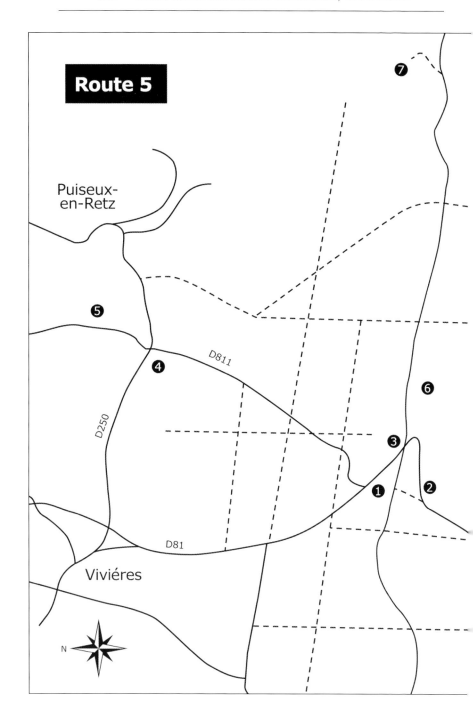

an early autumn dawn along the edge of the forest. There had been heavy dew smothering the ground and a thin drizzling rain had seemingly penetrated clothing and equipment. Colonel Morris – astride his horse – appeared to be everywhere at once. A man noted for his bravery and composure under fire, not ½ an hour before his death, after a period of sustained shellfire that had brought trees crashing down, he had called out to the men: 'D'you hear that? They're doing that to frighten you.' To which someone replied, 'If that's what they're after, they might as well stop. They succeeded with me hours ago.'

Lieutenant Colonel the Hon George Morris.

The German attack came from the north and it soon became apparent that this was no cavalry advanced guard but a much larger body of III Corps infantry supported by artillery. After the initial encounter had faded away – the Germans were clearly being cautious – Morris sent a runner to the 2/Coldstream lines ordering them to retire to a covering position along the railway line to the south. The line of retirement was through the forest to the west of the D811. Just as Morris and his Irish Guards were about to follow the Coldstream he received orders to remain in position until 1.00pm to allow the division to stop for lunch! Unable to recall the Coldstream, he remained in position and it was this unfortunate order that was responsible for the desperate fighting rearguard through the forest and the heavy toll in casualties incurred by the battalion. The brief respite in the German attack was soon continued. **Aubrey Herbert,** who was attached to the Irish Guards, described the Germans advancing towards their front and on the left flank at about 10.45am. 'There was a tremendous fire. The leaves, branches, etc, rained upon one. One's face was constantly fanned by the wind from their bullets'.

Return to your vehicle and retrace your route back to the Ronde de la Reine ❸. Travelling from this direction you can turn right at the forest crossroads along the minor road towards the Maison Forestière and park on the left. This forest road, running west–east through the forest,

The Ronde de la Reine where 2/Grenadier Guards had their headquarters. The forest road running off into the distance directly opposite leads to the Mangin Memorial.

is the line along which 2/Grenadiers and 3/Coldstream positioned themselves after falling back from the crossroads west of Puiseux. Where you are now is the approximate position of the Grenadiers' battalion headquarters, while No. 4 Company was along the road to the west, past the Maison Forestière, where it was in touch with 3/Coldstream. Across the road to the east the Grenadiers' Nos 1 and 2 Companies were along the rising ground about 75m south of the main ride ❻ which leads towards the **Mangin Memorial**. Altogether it was not a good spot for a fight with the dense undergrowth making communications difficult and fields of fire almost impossible to establish.

Attacked on all sides, the Irish had no choice but to fight a very costly running battle through the woods with the Germans almost on top of them. George Morris 'had a charmed life', wrote Aubrey Herbert. 'He raced from one place to another through the wood; cheering the men and chaffing them, and talking to me; smoking cigarette after cigarette.' Jeffreys remembered the Irish Guards had become involved in a running fight and withdrew with the Germans right on top of them. 'In this way they had come back on our left and the 3/Coldstream, so that there was very confused fighting at point blank range'. Company by company the Irish Guards fell back towards the Ronde de la Reine pursued by what **Major Bernard Gordon Lennox** described as 'the green Jaeger fellows'. At some point in their retirement Colonel Morris was killed, becoming the first ever commanding officer of the Irish Guards to fall in battle. Part of No. 4 Company counter-attacked from the Maison Forestière and it was during this bayonet charge that **Second Lieutenant George Cecil** and **Lieutenant the Hon John Manners** were killed. A third officer, **Lieutenant Buddy Needham**, was wounded and taken prisoner.

It was not long before the gaps on the left of the line were being exploited and fighting became a confused melee as German forces attempted to get round the left flank. Major Jeffreys: 'The first I heard of what was happening on my left was when Gerry Ruthven appeared leading a horse on which was the Brigadier [Scott-Kerr] badly wounded and obviously in great pain. He shouted to me that the enemy was held but we should shortly have to withdraw, and disappeared to the rear in the Forest'.

Command of the brigade now fell to **Lieutenant Colonel Noel Corry**, but taking over command of a brigade in these circumstances was well-nigh impossible and in truth no one was effectively in overall command as the battalions began to fall back to the bridge over the railway line north of Villers-Cotterêts – not an easy manoeuvre by any means. The Coldstream companies and Irish Guards were forced to fall back diagonally behind the Grenadiers – a manoeuvre made all the more difficult by the dense undergrowth. Major Bernard Gordon Lennox's No. 2 Company on the right of the line gave covering fire before they too began filtering back towards the railway:

> The firing on my left was very hot and the opposing forces were in some cases only 70 yards off each other . . . [then] the companies on my left were ordered off to the left to reinforce and I also sent one platoon along. Everyone was now mixed up hopelessly and officers just took command of whatever men they found. We now got the order to retire slowly on Villers-Cotterêts.

But this was not the end of the story. At around 1.00pm 6 Brigade, which had been posted to the south of Villers-Cotterêts, was ordered to form a defensive line through which the Guards could retire. As the guns of 70/Battery came into action a German advance began to compromise the gunners' positions, and two companies of 1/Royal Berkshire Regiment were ordered up to assist in limbering up the guns and holding back the hostile advance. **Sergeant Charles Meades** could only remember there being about fifty men to save six guns:

> We made a series of short rushes under heavy shrapnel fire until we were up to the guns. The Germans were about 800 yards away; and we could see them going down in scores . . . We fired all our ammunition, then a company of South Staffords reinforced us on the left flank and we saw the teams come up and fetch the guns.

The casualties
4 Guards Brigade suffered some 360 casualties in the Forêt de Retz, many of whom were left wounded and dying in the forest glades as the Guards fell back to Villers-Cotterêts. Some would not be discovered until it was too late; others like **Lieutenant John Manners** of the Grenadier Guards would not be formally identified at all, while the more fortunate fell into the hands of German ambulance units where they received attention. The fighting south of the town resulted in another 160 casualties. As many as eighty of the wounded were picked up by 4/ and 5/Field Ambulances and it was 4/Field Ambulance – many of whose men had already been taken prisoner at Landrecies – which established a dressing station in a nearby sugar factory. It was only next morning, after the medics realized that they had been left behind, that they narrowly escaped the fate of their comrades at Landrecies.

The Guards' Grave Cemetery
This is best approached on foot via the forest road leading down from the Maison Forestière. The cemetery is on the bend of the D81 and parking is practically impossible. Cross the road with care to the steps leading down to the cemetery, which was formed by the Irish Guards in November 1914 and contains ninety-eight casualties, of whom twenty are unidentified. Of the guardsmen buried here forty-five are Grenadiers, twenty-one are Irish Guards and eleven are from the Coldstream Guards. Only one man, **Private Mark Durkin** of 1/East Lancashire Regiment, was not a serving soldier in the Brigade of Guards.

The youngest soldier is a 17-year-old Grenadier Guardsman, **Lance Corporal Thomas Frederick Ayers**, and the oldest is 42-year-old **Lieutenant Colonel the Hon George Henry Morris** of the Irish Guards, who is buried side-by-side with **Second Lieutenant George Cecil** (2/Grenadier Guards), **Lieutenant Geoffrey Lambton** (2/Coldstream Guards) and **Major Charles Tisdsall** (1/Irish Guards). These four officers were eventually located and exhumed by George Morris's brother, Martin Henry Morris, 2nd Baron Killanin in November

Major Charles Tisdsall of the Irish Guards.

1914 after a previous attempt by Lady Violet Cecil to find her son's body had failed. Buried initially in a plot in the communal cemetery at Villers-Cotterêts, their remains were exhumed after the Armistice to be re-united with their men in the Guards Grave. Killanin's party also found ninety-four men, recorded their details where possible and re-buried them in the grave which later became the Guards' Grave Cemetery.

The Cecil Memorial

This imposing memorial is only a few metres from the Ronde de la Reine crossroads on the right-hand side of the road and was commissioned in 1922 by Lady Violet Cecil in memory of her son, George Edward Cecil of the Grenadier Guards. The inscription on the back of the memorial reads: 'In Honour of the officers and men of the Grenadier, Coldstream and Irish Guards who fell near this spot on 1st September 1914. This memorial was placed here by the mother of one of them and is especially dedicated to Second Lieutenant George Edward Cecil'. In 1978 the Grenadier Guards made arrangements for the memorial's future maintenance and transferred its upkeep to the CWGC.

The Mangin Memorial

Inaugurated in November 1926, the memorial commemorates the site of the Reaumont observatory tower erected on the orders of **General Charles Mangin** (1886–1925) at the time he commanded the Tenth French Army in July 1918. To reach the memorial walk along the ride from the Ronde de la Reine past the lone memorial to **Lieutenant Henri de Chasseval** – a reminder that the Forêt de Retz played an

The Guards' Grave Cemetery.

The Cecil Memorial.

important part in the Second Battle of the Marne in 1918 – until you are prompted by a signboard to leave the road and climb a small rise on the left where you will find the memorial ❼. To return to the Rond de la Reine either use the GR11A national footpath, which runs almost parallel to the ride you have just walked along, or retrace your steps. A map is useful.

Villers-Cotterêts French National Cemetery

The cemetery is to be found on the northwestern edge of the town on the D973 Route de Compiègne. It contains four casualties, one of which is unidentified; three of the graves are located on the right-hand side of the main central path, and the other is located on the rear left. Having fought in the rearguard action in the forest with 2/Grenadier Guards, the 23-year-old **Private James Heslin** of Hampstead in London died of his wounds in the French Auxiliary Hospital on 14 September 1914, as did **Private Hugh Williamson** of 8/Cameronians on 29 July 1918. The Canadian cavalryman **Private Richard Bradley** was serving with A Squadron of the Fort Garry Horse when he was killed during the March 1918 German offensive.

The Mangin Memorial.

Stage Four
Boursonne to Doue

This final stage of the guidebook covers the move south from Villers-Cotterêts to the BEF's crossing of the Marne at Meaux and then follows its route to La Ferté-sous-Jouarre. Although there were no specific actions such as those at Néry and Crépy-en-Valois after 1 September, the rearguards of the BEF were still in almost continual contact with the German advanced guard and these skirmishes took place right up to the Marne crossings and beyond. Our route follows I Corps to Meaux, on the way visiting three of the memorials and French cemeteries commemorating the Battle of the Marne (5–12 September 1914) before stopping off at the Great War Museum in Meaux. After visiting the Memorial to the Missing at La Ferté-sous-Jouarre we move south to Perreuse Château Franco-British Cemetery before concluding the retreat at the hilltop churchyard at Doue, where the Scots Greys witnessed the first manoeuvring by von Kluck's German First Army at the beginning of the Battle of the Marne.

Boursonne
After leaving Villers-Cotterêts the 2nd Division headed south towards the Marne along the D81 to the village of **Boursonne**, where 2/Grenadier Guards was ordered to take up a position in the village to cover the withdrawal of 4 and 6 Brigades. Take the same road out of Villers-Cotterêts – Avenue de Boursonne – which soon plunges into the Forêt Domaniale de Retz. As the road emerges from the forest a short distance from Boursonne, stop just after the single cottage on the right. At 6.00pm on 1 September 1914 the Grenadier Guards No. 3 Company was deployed astride the road between here and the northern outskirts of the village. **Captain Douglas Stephen** would have positioned his men as far as possible to cover the entrance to the village. We also know that **Major George Jeffreys** was here assessing the situation with **Major General Monro**; the two men were

discussing the fight to retrieve the 70/Battery guns. 'He stood (or rather sat on his horse) with us on the northerly outskirts of Boursonne', wrote Jeffreys in his diary. It was during this conversation that there was very nearly another case of friendly fire when 'out of the forest about 500 or 600 yards away to our left front appeared some cavalry riding quickly along and apparently going to pass our left flank'. Monro yelled out to the Grenadiers to change front and open fire. 'I was almost certain they were British', wrote Jeffreys, who 'ordered the platoon to change front, but not to open fire, and got my glasses onto them when I at once saw the grey horses of the Scots Greys'. Gradually 6 Brigade filtered through the forest passing the Grenadiers until the 2/Coldstream arrived bringing up the rear. Jeffreys notes that his battalion fell in behind, 'as there appeared to be no orders and we had been forgotten by our own brigade'.

Now continue into the village where the guards loopholed the garden walls and dug trenches in preparation for an attack. Jeffreys felt that 'after two hours work we had a reasonably strong position', but as had been the case on countless occasions before, orders arrived to abandon their positions and continue the march.

To follow in their footsteps continue through Boursonne – the road now becomes the D51 – and turn sharp left just before Ivors towards Autheuil-en-Valois on the D88. After approximately 3.5km, turn right on to the D18 towards Thury-en-Valois.

Arriving at **Thury-en-Valois**, where General Monro had established his Divisional Headquarters, Major Jeffreys was dismayed to find all the 4 Brigade supplies and transport were some 6km to the west at Betz. Apart from all the fighting in the forest the battalion had covered some 23km since 3.00am that morning and was exhausted. All the available accommodation had been taken up by 6 Brigade and there was nothing with which to provide a meal for the men. Jeffreys raised the roof and eventually demanded to see Monro, who made immediate arrangements for rations to be provided. A ration dump 1.6km outside the village on the D77 towards **Villeneuve-sous-Thury** provided the necessary bully beef, biscuit and jam. 'Then the battalion just lay down by the road and slept. There was a farmhouse close by and (having issued orders that we would march at 2am to join the brigade) I and Stephen went in and groped our way into pitch dark room full of sleeping humanity of sorts and found a vacant corner and slept'.

Just before first light the next morning the battalion marched back to Thury as 12/Lancers were setting fire to the remaining supplies at the ration dump. Jeffreys tells us they were reunited with the brigade at **Betz** before pressing on to **Puiseux**, where the battalion breakfasted.

> *From Thury-en-Valois take the D922 west in the direction of Antilly and then on to Betz.*

Betz

As the Grenadiers marched through the village they would have passed the gates of the chateau on the main street, the Rue de la Libération. The chateau had been occupied by the ambulance units of 5/Field Ambulance which had moved to the village the previous day with the wounded from the fighting around Villers-Cotterêts. The **Revd Frederick Smithwick**, who was attached to the ambulance unit, recalled they established a field hospital,

The entrance to the chateau at Betz where 5/Field Ambulance established a temporary field hospital.

The French National Cemetery on the D332 outside Betz.

in a lovely château there. Bearers went [back] towards the battlefield to bring in the wounded. All through the night the wounded were being brought in till we had about 150, including General Scott-Kerr of the Guards Brigade, Lt Desmond Fitzgerald and Captain Burton, Irish Guards. They were medically attended and put on hay in some of the large barns of the château.

Unfortunately Smithwick's chateau is now owned by the King of Morocco, Mohammed VI, and no visiting is allowed.

Moving ever southward to follow the line of the BEF's Retreat, take the D332 from Betz. In a little over a kilometre you will come to the **Betz French National Cemetery** on the right. The cemetery with its central memorial stone is the first of numerous memorials connected with the Battle of the Marne which we pass on the way to Meaux. Drive on to Acy-en-Multien then take the D18 to the hamlet of

Nogeon. Bear left on to the D51/D38 to Puiseux and stay on the road to reach Barcy, which lies some 15km to the southwest of Betz.

Although outside the scope of this guidebook, you will find the **Monument Notre-Dame de la Marne** at Barcy – east of the village on the D97 – and the French and German Cemeteries at **Chambry –** just 1.5km along the same road for the French and only ½km further on for the German – worthy of a visit. The German dead at Chambry are casualties of the Battle of the Ourq, while in the French cemetery 1,258 soldiers are remembered with the standard concrete cross – many of which are showing signs of wear.

The Monument Notre-Dame de la Marne near Barcy.

From Barcy head south along the D38 towards Meaux and pick up the signs for Musée de Grande Guerre.

Meaux and the Marne crossings

On 2 September 26/Field Company arrived at Meaux at 6.30am. The company had just marched 64km/40 miles in a little over 24 hours and were anticipating a rest. **Major Harry Pritchard** had only just shut his eyes when he was roused by Brigadier General Fowke who arrived with orders for the Marne bridges to be prepared and blown. The bridges allocated to 26/Field Company were but a small part of the wider operational order issued by GHQ later on 2 September. Early on 3 September the BEF crossed the Marne along a 48km/30-mile-wide front. The 1st Division crossed at **Trilport**, the 2nd and 3rd Divisions at **Meaux** and the 4th and 5th Divisions further west at **Villenoy** and **Lagny-sur-Marne** respectively. At **Villenoy** the road to the bridge on the southern bank rises steeply – any vehicle driving at speed would not realize the bridge had been destroyed until it was too late. Witnessed by two Irish Guardsmen who had been stranded on the opposite bank, a car plunged headlong through the gap in the bridge and thence into the river. It was said at the time the car was driven by a German spy attempting to return to German lines. The fate of the driver was not recorded. Much of Allenby's cavalry crossed at **Gournay**, which was practically in the Paris suburbs, a stark reminder of just how close to the French capital the fighting had progressed. After the 2nd Division had passed through Meaux, 5/Field Company blew the road and railway bridges successfully and 57/Field Company destroyed all the other bridges, weirs, barges and boats between Villenoy and Trilport.

Musée de Grande Guerre Pays de Meaux

Signs for the museum abound on most of the northern approaches to Meaux. If you are using a sat nav, the address is Route de Varreddes which is off the D405. The museum was opened on 11 November 2011 and is housed in a slender, modernistic building designed by the French architect Christophe Lab. Outside is the huge 25m-tall 'American Monument', an ornately writhing figure of Liberty entwined with the dead and dying by sculptor Frederick Mac Monnies which was erected in 1932 by the American Friends of

A Bleriot XI Militaire aircraft displayed in La Musée de Grande Guerre at Meaux.

Trench reconstruction at La Musée de Grande Guerre at Meaux.

France in the presence of French President Albert Lebrun to commemorate the First Battle of the Marne. The monument is sometimes referred to as the statue of 'tearful liberty'. Inside there is plenty to interest the British and Commonwealth visitor and although the displays lean towards the French story of the Great War, the reconstructions of French and German trenches and the emphasis on the myriad collection of uniforms, equipment and weaponry worn and used by both sides is guaranteed to hold the interest of most. At the time of writing the price for entry is €10 per adult, €7 for students, military veterans and senior citizens and children up to the age of 8 are free. A family ticket for two adults and two children under 18 costs €25. As usual, please check with the museum for up-to-date information on prices and opening times before visiting; www.museedelagrande guerre.eu/en.

> *If you intend visiting the communal cemetery, the following directions from the museum may help. Leave the museum car park and continue into Meaux along the D2405. Just after passing over the Canal de l'Ourcq you will see the cemetery on the right. Continue to pass beneath the railway line and drive for another 500m to the major junction with traffic lights then take the turning on the right – Avenue de la République. Drive along the one-way street and continue straight over at the six-way intersection with traffic lights to the next crossroads. Turn right here on to Rue Jean Jaurès which will take you through a narrow tunnel under the railway line. You will find the cemetery at the end of the next right turn down an avenue of trees.*

Meaux New Communal Cemetery

The military plot is in the southeastern corner of the cemetery where there is one casualty of the retreat to which is attached a most intriguing story. **Lieutenant Alastair Smith-Cumming** of 1/Seaforth Highlanders was serving on the general staff when he died in an accident on 30 September 1914. He was the son of **Captain** (Royal Navy) **Sir George Mansfield Smith-Cumming** (1859–1923), who was the first director of what would become the Secret Intelligence Service (SIS), also known as MI6. In this role Sir George was particularly successful in building a post-imperial intelligence service. In 1914, he was involved in a serious road accident in France, in which his son

Alastair was killed. Legend has it that in order to escape the car wreck he was forced to amputate his own foot using a pen knife. Hospital records have shown, however, that while both his legs were broken, his left foot was only amputated the day after the accident. Smith-Cumming was the basis for 'Control', the fictional head of the SIS in the John le Carré espionage novel *Tinker, Tailor, Soldier, Spy*. In the big-screen version Control signs his name as 'C' using green ink just as Smith-Cumming did in real life. In the television series *Reilly, Ace of Spies*, he was portrayed by Norman Rodway. The question is, what exactly was Alastair Smith-Cumming doing with his father on the day he was killed and was he a spy working for his father? Also buried here are 24-year-old **Private Charles Dahman** and 18-year-old **Private Henry Mason**. Both men were killed in 1918.

La Ferté-sous-Jouarre

With the Marne behind them, the troops of I Corps turned east and marched to La Ferté-sous-Jouarre, where Major Pritchard's sappers had two bridges to destroy: a large stone-arched bridge and a steel bridge a little further upstream comprising six arched girders. With both bridges ready by 6.45pm on 3 September, counter orders then arrived with instructions to remove the charges and leave the bridges intact. Pritchard – by now wise to the inconsistent nature of divisional orders when it came to blowing bridges – ignored the instruction to withdraw the charges and posted his men on the two bridges to await developments. It was just as well he did – at 4.00am on 4 September the immediate destruction of the bridges was ordered. **Lieutenant A G Smith** successfully blew the stone-arched bridge – on the site of the modern-day Pont de l'Europe – but **Lieutenant Earle Calthrop's** bridge was left standing despite the girders being cut through by the charges. As Calthrop moved across the bridge to inspect the damage German cavalry arrived on the northern bank and opened fire. Fortunately Nos 2 and 3 Companies of 1/Coldstream Guards under the command of **Major C J C Grant** had been deployed as rearguard and their rifle fire drove the enemy horsemen off, but time was running out. After a second attempt to blow the bridge also failed, the rearguard was ordered to retire and 4 hours later – much to the disgust of the Coldstream Guards – a German battalion crossed the Marne using the bridge.

> *From the cemetery retrace your route to the six-way junction and take the second right one-way street – Rue Noefort – to the T-junction ahead and turn left on to the Rue Faubourg Saint-Nicolas. At the major crossroads with lights ahead go straight across, following signs for the A4 motorway, Chateau Thierry, La Ferté-sous-Jouarre and Trilport. Continue and leave Meaux, crossing the Marne at Trilport just as the BEF's 1st Division did. Continue through Saint-Jean-les-Deux-Jumeaux and Sammeron. As you approach La Ferté-sous-Jouarre from the direction of Sammeron, the large Memorial to the Missing is off to the left on the first roundabout you come to as you enter the town. Take the first turning on the right – Rue du Petit Morin – and after parking your vehicle walk up to the roundabout.*

The Memorial to the Missing of the Marne
The memorial was built on land given by **Adrien Fizeau**, former mayor of Jouarre, in memory of his father. The Fizeau connection is commemorated with bilingual inscriptions to either side of the steps leading up to the river-facing side of the memorial. Unveiled on 4 November 1928 by Sir William Pulteney who commanded III Corps in 1914, the memorial commemorates the 3,740 officers and men of the BEF who fell at the battles of Mons, Le Cateau, the Marne and the Aisne between the end of August and early October 1914 and have no known graves. At the four corners of the pavement on which the monument stands are stone columns supporting urns which bear the coats of arms of the four constituent nations of the United Kingdom. The memorial was designed by **George Hartley Goldsmith**, a decorated veteran of the Western Front. For those of you wishing to view the register you will find it is now kept at the mairie and is only available for consultation during working hours.

The Royal Engineers Memorials
From the Memorial to the Missing walk towards the river and under the road bridge, ahead of you is the first of two identical obelisks marking the site of a pontoon bridge erected during the advance to the Aisne on 9/10 September 1914 by 9/Field Company alongside the very bridge which 26/Field Company had destroyed a week earlier! Look across the river and you will see the second of the two memorials. The bridge was 218ft long and was constructed mainly from material found locally.

The Memorial to the Missing at La Ferté-sous-Jouarre.

The two Royal Engineers Memorials at La Ferté-sous-Jouarre marking the spot on either bank where 9/Field Company built their bridge to span the River Marne.

Jardin du Lieutenant James Collingwood-Thompson

Behind the Memorial to the Missing is the garden dedicated to Edward James Vibart Collingwood-Thompson. Collingwood-Thompson was the first officer of 2/Royal Welch Fusiliers to be killed in action, an event that occurred nearby on 9 September when he was fatally wounded during the battalion's advance towards the Aisne. A private memorial, which was erected by his mother and is notoriously difficult to locate, marks the exact spot where he was wounded and can be found some 500m further east. The more scenic route to find it is to head down the Rue Fizeau/Quai des Anglais towards the river from the Memorial to the Missing – keeping the gardens on your left – for approximately 420m until you reach the junction with the Rue des Carreaux on your right. Walk up this street to the junction with the Rue de Conde (D402) and you will see a cast metal plaque on the gable end of the last house on the right bearing the inscription in English and French 'Here Lieutenant J Collingwood Thompson 2nd Battalion Royal Welch Fusiliers was mortally wounded September 9th 1914. He died fighting for the right and honour of England and France.' On the street corner below it there is also a small dwarf obelisk at ground level bearing the inscription 'Lieutenant J Collingwood Thompson 2nd Battalion Royal Welch Fusiliers who fell here September 9th Mortally wounded buried in the Military Cemetery Perreuse Jouarre'. We will visit the cemetery in which Collingwood-Thompson is buried a little later.

> *Retrace your route back towards Meaux and turn left at the main junction with lights on to the D402 following signs for Coulommiers and Jouarre. Just after entering Jouarre turn right at the intersection – you will see a green CWGC sign at low level – to drive along the Rue des Belles Dames to find the communal cemetery on the right.*

La Ferté-sous-Jouarre Communal Cemetery

Although not technically casualties of the Retreat, the five men buried here in the southeastern section of the cemetery will always welcome a visit. All were most probably casualties of the advance to the Aisne and were either killed during that advance or died of wounds received. **Driver John Reid** of 70/Battery probably fought at Villers-Cotterêts on 1 September, while **Private James Finch** of 1/Hampshires would have been among the battalion waiting for orders at Carlepont on 30 August.

Private Llewellyn Roberts of 2/Royal Welch Fusiliers and Sergeant Samuel Newton of 1/East Lancashires may well have been casualties of the same engagement at La Ferté-sous-Jouarre in which Lieutenant Collingwood-Thompson was wounded.

> *Leave the cemetery and at the mini-roundabout ahead take the second right on to the D114P towards Signy-Signets and Les Corbiers. Pass through Les Corbiers keeping a sharp look-out for the green CWGC signs – and at the far end of the village bear left. The road bends at right angles to the right – towards the Étang de Perreuse and the Château de Pereuse. Just as you approach the wood which surrounds the lake you should pick up the last CWGC signpost for the cemetery, which you will find some 300m down a track to your left.*

Perreuse Château Franco-British Cemetery

This cemetery is situated within the grounds of the Perreuse Château, and is approached along a track that is suitable for most vehicles. The chateau was used by French medical units throughout the war and the site of the cemetery was donated by the owner, Madame Dumez. Of the 150 Commonwealth dead buried here only 47 are victims of the 1914 fighting and most of these are casualties from the advance to the Aisne, which took place after 5 September. There are five definite casualties of the Retreat buried here: 35-year-old Captain Stephen Christy (I.D.25) of C Squadron, 20/Hussars, who was killed at the Ussy bridgehead covering the retirement of B Squadron on 3 September. Wounded at Crépy-en-Valois while in command of C Company was 41-year-old Major Percy Hastings (I.C.4) of 1/Queen's Own Royal West Kents. If you visited the site of the Crépy rearguard in Stage Three, you may have stood on the very ground on which he received his wounds. Birmingham-born Private Henry Lewis (I.B.18) was 28 years old when he was killed serving with 2/South Staffordshire Regiment on 2 September. There are three cavalrymen from 2/Dragoons (Royal Scots Greys) buried together (I.B.37–9), all victims of the cavalry action at Rebais when a troop of the Greys, cut off from the regiment by the advancing Germans, attempted to 'run the gauntlet' through the town. 'At the head of his men Captain [Thomas Edmund Sotherton] Estcourt dashed into the street. His horse however slipped upon the cobbles and came down with him almost at

Perreuse Château Franco-British Cemetery.

once, and while he was lying stunned, he was seized and taken prisoner. Of the whole troop, only five men and eight horses escaped back to the regiment'. Retired from the army in 1919 due to ill-health from injuries and the privations of captivity, Estcourt was elected to Parliament as the Conservative MP for Pontefract, West Yorkshire in the general election of 1931. He lost his seat in 1935 to the Labour candidate.

The French liaison officer, 35-year-old **Captain Jean-Marie Pierre de Mas-Latrie**, the son of the commander of the French XVIII Corps, was also killed during this action and his headstone is along the wall. Here you will also find 20-year-old **Second Lieutenant Edward Collingwood-Thompson** (I.D.46) of 2/Royal Welch Fusiliers. He died on 10 September of wounds received the previous day. There are also sixteen Second World War burials, most of which are aircrew brought in from the surrounding area, but one of them does have an aura of mystery surrounding it. In plot 2, row c, grave 46 lies **Lieutenant Eric Joseph Denis Cauchi**. His regiment is given as 'general list' but in fact he was a F Section agent of the highly secretive Special Operations Executive (SOE), acting as part of a network of agents operating behind German lines. Cauchi went by the name of 'Pedro' as part of the 'Stockbroker' circuit but he was caught and executed by the Germans on 5 February 1944. His name is included on the Valencay SOE Memorial in the Indre Département. The monument, which cost £50,000, was inaugurated on 6 May 1991 – the fiftieth anniversary of the first F Section agent being sent to France – in the presence of Her Majesty Queen Elizabeth the Queen Mother.

> *Our final stop is at Doue, which is about 20 minutes to the southeast. It is best approached by continuing along the D114P towards Signy-Signets and turning left at the junction with the D21. After a little over 3km turn left onto the D19 which will take you into Doue.*

The village of Doue is dominated to the north by the Butte de Doue which stands above the surrounding flat plain. On 3 September 1914, 5 Cavalry Brigade established its temporary headquarters in the village before retiring towards Coulommiers. 20/Hussars was detailed as rearguard to the brigade which it covered with B Squadron and its machine-gun section, which, as recorded in the 15/Hussars' history, 'took up a strong position on the hill by the church and got shelled as we were leaving'.

The butte has long been a place of worship and the Church of St Martin on its lower slope was completed in the late thirteenth century. Classed as an historic monument in 1922, the restoration of this fine building was begun in 1965 by the Conservation Régionale des Bâtiments de France. The butte is easily approached by car from the village, there is ample parking at the top and the view is exceptionally fine, which is probably why a cavalry patrol from C Squadron of the Scots Greys found themselves on the butte on 5 September – the final day of the retreat from Mons. Looking east towards the high ground on the far side of the Petit Morin, they could see a huge troop movement taking place, as recorded in the Scots Greys' history: 'From here could be seen three long columns of Germans, but instead of moving against the British they were moving

The Butte de Doue from where the Scots Greys observed the opening manoeuvres of the Battle of the Marne.

The thirteenth-century church of St Martin at the Butte de Doue where Corporal Stuart Barnett is buried in the churchyard.

in a south south-easterly direction across our front.' This, of course, was von Kluck with his main army, who having left his 4th Reserve Corps with a cavalry division to contain the French Sixth Army forming round Paris, was moving to join von Bülow operating against the French Fifth Army, thinking that the British Army was too negligible as a fighting force 'to be worth troubling about'. What they were witnessing were the opening moves of the Battle of the Marne. The Retreat from Mons was well and truly finished as it was on that same day that the slow advance to the Aisne began. Before you leave walk round to the communal cemetery entrance and pay a visit to **Corporal Stuart Barnett** from Surbiton in Surrey, whose grave is located to the northwest end. He was killed in this vicinity on 7 September 1914 serving with the Royal Engineers Signal Company and is the only CWGC burial in the cemetery.

Further Reading

In addition to the companion volume to this guide – *The Retreat From Mons – North* – a number of titles have appeared in recent years which cover some of the routes presented. Several of the **Battleground Europe** titles published by Pen and Sword focus on aspects of the Retreat and provide further detail for the interested reader. To date there are three titles relevant to this guide:

Cave, Nigel and Sheldon, Jack, *Le Cateau*, Pen and Sword, 2008
Horsfall, Jack and Cave, Nigel, *Mons 1914*, Pen and Sword, 2000
Takle, Patrick, *The Affair at Néry*, Pen and Sword, 2006

Aspects of the Retreat are also covered in Rose Coombs' seminal guide *Before Endeavours Fade* (After the Battle Publications, 2006), and Major and Mrs Holt's Battlefield Guide *The Western Front – North* (Pen and Sword, 2007). Both these guidebooks are primarily written for tourists using a vehicle to explore the area. Osprey Publishing has produced a comprehensive series of Great War books which includes some very informative titles about the various expeditionary forces of the Allied armies and a mini-series covering the German Army. Of particular note is Bruce Gudmundsson's *The British Expeditionary Force 1914–15* (Osprey, 2005). The following three books are always useful as reference: Gerald Gliddon's *VCs Handbook, The Western Front 1914–1918* (Sutton, 2005), and his updated single volume covering the first year, *VCs of the First World War, 1914* (History Press, 2011), along with Martin Middlebrook's excellent guide to British Army infantry divisions, *Your Country Needs You* (Pen and Sword, 2000).

For battlefield visitors who wish to expand their knowledge of the retreat in more depth, the following may be of interest:

Ascoli, David, *The Mons Star*, Harrap, 1981
Craster, J M, *Fifteen Rounds a Minute*, Macmillan, 1976
Holmes, Richard, *Riding the Retreat*, Jonathan Cape, 1995
Murland, Jerry, *Retreat and Rearguard 1914*, Pen and Sword, 2011
Terraine, John, *Mons Retreat to Victory*, Batsford, 1960

Index